SOG MEDIC

SOG MEDIC

Stories from Vietnam and Over the Fence

JOE PARNAR AND ROBERT DUMONT

CASEMATE

Philadelphia & Oxford

First published in 2018.
This edition published in the United States of America and in the United Kingdom in 2023 by
CASEMATE PUBLISHERS
1950 Lawrence Road, Havertown, PA 19083, USA
and
The Old Music Hall, 106–108 Cowley Road, Oxford OX4 1JE, UK

First published by Paladin Press in 2007

Paperback Edition: ISBN 978-1-63624-320-7
Digital Edition: ISBN 978-1-61200-634-5 (ePub)

A CIP record for this book is available from the British Library

Printed and bound in the United States of America by Integrated Books International

Typeset in India by Versatile PreMedia Services. www.versatilepremedia.com

For a complete list of Casemate titles, please contact:

CASEMATE PUBLISHERS (US)
Telephone (610) 853-9131
Fax (610) 853-9146
Email: casemate@casematepublishers.com
www.casematepublishers.com

CASEMATE PUBLISHERS (UK)
Telephone (0)1226 734350
Email: casemate-uk@casematepublishers.co.uk
www.casematepublishers.co.uk

This book is dedicated to all the brave warriors who fought
with SOG and to the memory of:
Craig Davis, July 6, 1946–May 11, 2007, my brother in arms.

"There was a consciousness always of the presence of his comrades about him. He felt the subtle battle brotherhood more potent even than the cause for which they were fighting. It was a mysterious fraternity born of the smoke and danger of death."

Stephen Crane, *The Red Badge of Courage*

Contents

Preface

The authors would like to thank Casemate for publishing this 2018 edition of SOG Medic. With additional text, maps, and photos, we hope it finds a wide audience of new readers and previous readers will wish to re-acquaint themselves with the book in a new format.

One of the most gratifying results since the book's first publication in 2007 has been the number of people that have contacted us regarding various events chronicled in the original narrative. We've been in touch with several individuals who were mentioned by name and communicated with them at greater length, thus enabling us to expand on various topics. Lee Swain, Paul Renner, William Groves, Tony Dorff, and Steve Roche are among these folks. In other instances, when the names were unknown to the authors at the time of the book's first writing, we have since learned who several people were and what units they were assigned to. This is the case with Huey pilot Kent Harper and Cobra pilot Gary Higgins, both of whom played significant roles in the events depicted in Chapter 17—… "The Loss of Ben Ide." Similarly, helicopter pilots Craig Collier and Carl Hoeck and their crews, along with covey rider Mike Bingo, were key players providing essential air support for the SLAM operation recounted in Chapter 16.

There have also been instances when family members of persons killed in combat actions have come forward and expressed their gratitude for our relating the circumstances of those actions and memorializing their lost loved ones. Randy Ide and Alan Apperson are two examples, as well as the family of John Kedenburg.

We are especially pleased that the editors have chosen the image of Medal of Honor recipient John Kedenburg and his team for the cover of the new edition of SOG Medic. The photo was taken by George Wilson Hunt who accompanied RT-Nevada on an in-country mission in May 1968—a few weeks before John was killed in Laos. A second photo taken by Sgt. Hunt during that mission is to be found in Chapter 6. The events surrounding the loss of John Kedenburg are covered in somewhat greater detail in this edition as we have discovered further information. Hunt's arresting photos and Joe's vivid memories provide a fitting tribute to their fallen comrade.

Joe Parnar
Robert Dumont

Foreword

Over the years since the Vietnam War, a then-classified U.S. Army unit known as SOG (Studies and Observations Group) has spawned a large number of individual myths, legends, and war stories. Few match the varied perspectives and detailed recall of Special Forces medic Joe Parnar.

Joe served with SOG during 1968 and 1969 in the provincial capital city of Kontum near the tri-border area that gave the SOG commandos operating there access to the forbidden areas of Laos and Cambodia. During his tour with SOG, he served as dispensary medic, chase medic, Hatchet Force medic, and as a recon team member. This gives him an active voice and direct experience not only in an unusual number of combat roles but also in dealing with and treating the civilians and indigenous peoples of that area.

I first met Joe several years ago when doing research for my photo history book of SOG at CCC, *Running Recon: A Photo History of SOG Special Ops along the Ho Chi Minh Trail* (Paladin Press, 2004). He had left the SOG compound near Kontum called Command and Control Central about a month before I got there in April 1969. In looking for additional photographs for my own book, I was put in touch with Joe by a SOG memorabilia collector, and he generously allowed me the use of his photographs in my book. In speaking with Joe about our experiences in Vietnam, I was struck by the breadth of his experience and his ability to tell stories that provided real background and texture to his experiences, a vivid picture of what those experiences were like. He has an authentic voice, and he adds much to the life and corroboration of a unit that has, because of the secretive nature of its work, very little official documentation.

Thus, I am greatly pleased that Joe has taken the time to put down all his experiences in this book, for they are an important contribution to the history of SOG. At the same time, they sustain the myth of SOG exploits, the unique nature of its activities, and the extraordinary character of many of the men who served there. Joe speaks with a certain candor that may make some people uncomfortable; he doesn't clean it up to make it more acceptable—he tells it as he remembers it.

Joe's stories also remind me of something that I didn't pay a lot of attention to at the time, namely the enormous responsibility and burden that a medic carries. He has to not only keep himself alive and functioning, but at the same time he has to take care of the wounded and suffering. When everyone else takes a break to rest or eat, he treats the wounded. When engaged in a firefight with the enemy, he doesn't stay down, he gets up and treats the wounded. When settling down at night, when others are resting or sleeping, he treats the wounded. And sometimes, after having returned to the FOB, he has the final duty, the privilege, of preparing the bodies of our dead for return to their families back home in the United States. These stories are not only a testimony to Joe's efforts but also are part of the universal story of all medics who have served our troops, indeed all troops, throughout history. And to this day, Special Forces medics continue to carry out that tradition in all the corners of the world.

One of the problems of war stories is that they are often difficult to corroborate, or have some aspect that make them seem suspect, or at least exaggerated, and I wanted to be as truthful and accurate as I could be when doing my book. Joe's recall is detailed and accurate, and it is also important to him that it be right. What I could check always corroborated with what he had to say, in fact, if not in perspective. In Joe and in this book, those two linchpins of relevant war stories, memory and perspective, are well met. This doesn't mean that everyone who was there will agree with him; it means that he has the right to tell his experiences.

Joe was patiently aided in these efforts to get his stories in print by the abilities of wordsmith Bob Dumont. It is a difficult job to get the words to flow smoothly while at the same time maintaining the authenticity of the speaker's voice, and Bob has done that well. Simply put, good teamwork has produced this excellent book.

If you would know about the Vietnam War, about SOG, about being a Special Forces medic, or just about war and warriors, read this book. Along the way you will meet Joe Parnar and a number of his fellow SOG members who define what it took to be extraordinary men in challenging circumstances.

Frank Greco

Acknowledgments

There are many people who inspired me to write this book. Ray Harris provided the initial thrust with his pioneering work *Break Contact, Continue Mission* (Paladin Press, 1990). Although presented as fiction, anyone who served in SOG will attest that it contains far more fact than fiction.

I am indebted to John L. Plaster, Major (U.S. Army, retired) for the example of his definitive works, *SOG: The Secret Wars of America's Commandos in Vietnam* (Simon & Schuster, 1997); *SOG: A Photo History of the Secret Wars* (Paladin Press, 2000); and *Secret Commandos: Behind Enemy Lines with the Elite Warriors of SOG* (Simon & Schuster, 2004). These books led to the declassification of much of the government's restrictions on SOG operations and have made my book possible.

Much credit also goes to Frank Greco, author of *Running Recon: A Photo Journey with SOG Special Ops Along the Ho Chi Minh Trail* (Paladin Press, 2004); and *Kontum: Command and Control* (Xlibris Press, 2005). He encouraged me greatly and gave me further impetus by including two of my eyewitness accounts in *Running Recon* and assisted in proofreading the original draft of my journal.

SOG memorabilia collector and author Jason Hardy also aided me considerably with his countless contacts with SOG veterans and brought me together with numerous persons who refreshed my memory and put names to many of the individuals depicted in this work.

Special thanks go out to Luke Dove, who provided photos and put me in touch with Jim Williams (Panther 033), pilot with the 361st Aviation Company (The Pink Panthers), who in turn provided me with the names of many of the helicopter crews who participated in our missions. I was never aware of the names of the crew members when the incidents happened, and Jim was able to give identities to those who so heroically supported SOG operations. Without them, recon along the Ho Chi Minh Trail would have been almost impossible and nearly suicidal.

Craig Davis, Paul Morris, Robert Kotin, and Bryon Loucks supplied many photos used in this book. Craig's uncanny memory for details and the names of individuals involved in these accounts was invaluable to me.

John (Tilt) Meyer was inspirational with his early accounts of SOG missions published over the years in *Soldier of Fortune* magazine and in his book, *Across the Fence: The Secret War in Vietnam* (Real War Stories, 2003; expanded edition published 2013, SOG Books).

I am also very grateful to Gerald Denison for sharing his recollections of June 13, 1968, concerning the location and other details of the extraction of RT Nevada.

I would especially like to thank my protégé, Kyle Davidson, for his patience with me in devoting so much time to this project and for his support in overcoming the countless computer problems I experienced.

Finally, I would like to thank Robert Dumont, who edited and literally rewrote parts of my journal, making it far more readable and understandable to those who have no military exposure. Many times, those of us involved in military units take for granted that everyone is familiar with jargon, terms, and expressions used in our everyday experiences. Bob's efforts have helped me overcome many of these difficulties and resulted in a far more readable and flowing narrative.

Glossary

Arc Light—Code name for B-52 bombing raid.

ARVN—Army of the Republic of Vietnam. The regular South Vietnamese army.

Bird Dog—Cessna O-1 single-engine reconnaissance planes used by FAC and SPAF pilots to support SOG operations.

Bright Light—Code name for emergency rescue missions to recover downed pilots or provide assistance to recon teams in trouble.

C-3—Amber-colored plastic explosive available at the FOBs. Used less extensively than C-4 because of its oily nature.

C-4—A white plastic explosive having the appearance of window putty. Used both as an explosive and as a supply of heat for cooking as it burned with no smoke and without exploding.

CAR-15—A version of the M-16 with shorter barrel and collapsible stock preferred by most recon team members. Fired same .223-caliber ammunition as the M-16.

CCC/Command and Control Central—SOG field command established in 1968 as expansion of FOB2 at Kontum with launch site at Dak To. Operations from CCC were conducted in tri-border regions of Laos, Cambodia, and Vietnam.

CCN/Command and Control North—Largest of the three MACV-SOG field commands, created in late 1967. An expansion of FOB4 located at Da Nang near Marble Mountain. It included launch sites previously established at Hue-Phu Bai (FOB1); Khe Sanh (FOB3), which by August 1968 was no longer operational; and Kham Duc. Missions initiated from CCN took place primarily in Laos and the DMZ (Demilitarized Zone).

CCS/Command and Control South—Newest SOG field command, located at Ban Me Thuot (FOB5). Operations launched from CCS were carried out in central Cambodia or VC-dominated areas of South Vietnam.

Charlie—Term used to describe the Communist forces operating in Vietnam. Loosely applied to both the NVA and the Vietcong.

Charlie Model Gunship—Modified Huey helicopters (aka Hogs) outfitted with rocket pods, mini-guns, and machine guns. Had a crew of four—pilot/aircraft commander, co-pilot/gunner, crew chief, and door gunner. Crew chief and door gunners generally had M-60 machine guns although some models had crew-controlled side-firing mini-guns. Also, a "Frog" version that had a nose turret with 40mm grenade launcher mounted.

CIDG—Civilian Irregular Defense Group. Non-professional civil and village defense militia comprised primarily of ethnic minority members and trained by U.S. Special Forces.

Claymore—Small antipersonnel mines, hand detonated by wire, that were used by SOG teams to provide security in RONs or to ambush enemy troops.

Cluster Bomb Unit (CBU)—Anti-personnel anti-armor munition that when launched or dropped releases and disperses explosive sub-munitions (bomblets) over a wide area.

Cobra—Bell AH-1 helicopter gunships that supported SOG missions. First appeared at FOB2 in August, 1968. Cobras had a crew of two—pilot/aircraft commander and co-pilot/gunner. Had a faster cruising speed and a narrower front profile than Charlie Model gunships. Armament consisted of side-mounted rocket pods, mini-guns, cannon, and nose-turret-mounted dual mini-guns or single mini-gun with M129 40mm grenade launcher.

Covey—Code name for U.S. Air Force pilots of the Cessna 0-1 Bird Dog, O-2 Super Skymaster, and North American Rockwell OV-10 Bronco observation aircraft, that acted as Command and Control ships coordinating air assets and movements of teams on the ground for SOG missions. Bird Dog 0-1s were piloted by SPAF (Sneaky Pete Air Force) pilots.

Covey Rider—Typically an ex-recon One-Zero who flew with the SPAF or Covey Pilot to coordinate communication with the recon teams on the ground.

Daniel Boone—Code name used to designate cross border missions into Cambodia.

Degar—See **Montagnards.**

DEROS—Date of Estimated Return from Overseas.

Det Cord—Primacord, an explosive that resembled a length of cord. Came in 150-foot coils and used to connect demolition charges.

Eldest Son—Code name used to describe booby-trapped AK-47 and mortar ammunition. See also **Italian Green**.

FAC—Forward Air Controller.

Fast Mover—Jet aircraft.

FOB—Forward Operations Base.

Hare—Code name used by medics at Dak To to describe Huey gunships when talking to Covey.

Hatchet Force/Hatchet Platoon—A Hatchet Force consisted of a battalion of indigenous personnel led by Americans. The battalion was made up of four SLAM companies, and each SLAM Company was made up of three Hatchet Platoons. The platoons were designed to go to the aid of recon teams or attack suitable targets found by the teams.

Huey—Bell UH-1 utility helicopters used in support of SOG operations. There were both passenger carrying (slicks) and gunship versions.

Indigenous Personnel—Term used to describe civilians hired by the FOBs to conduct missions. They could be Vietnamese, Montagnard, Nung, Laotian, Cambodians, or ex-NVA.

Italian Green—Code name for booby-trapped AK-47 and mortar rounds doctored to explode prematurely, injuring or killing the users. Normally planted in enemy caches or along trails. See also **Eldest Son**.

KIA—Killed in action.

Kingbee—Sikorsky CH-34 helicopters piloted by Vietnamese pilots used in support of SOG operations.

Klondike—Radio relay site established in March/April 1969 after Sledgehammer was closed in February/March 1969. Provided a commo link from RTs in Cambodia with FOB2. Located on Hill

1152, four to five kilometers east-southeast of the 'Yard camp at coordinates AR811801.

Leghorn—Permanently manned radio relay site located on a mountaintop approximately eight miles inside Laos.

Leg—A put-down used to refer to those who were not airborne or jump qualified.

LLDB—Luc Luong Dac Biet— South Vietnamese Army Special Forces.

LZ—Helicopter landing zone.

LZ Mary Lou—4th Division firebase located three to four kilometers south of FOB2 off the west side of Highway 14 at coordinates ZA22958293. Housed 1/35 Inf., 1/10 Cav., & 1/92 Arty. Had X-ray capabilities available to FOB2 medics.

M-16—The standard rifle issued to U.S. troops in Vietnam. Fired .223-caliber ammunition.

M-79—The 40mm shotgun-like grenade launcher used by U.S. troops in Vietnam.

MACV-SOG—Military Assistance Command Vietnam-Studies and Observations Group.

McGuire Rig Extraction—Exfiltration of recon teams using four ropes dropped from helicopters onto which recon teams connected and were lifted from openings in the jungle and flown back to Vietnam while suspended below the helicopters.

MIA—Missing in action.

Montagnard ('Yard)—French name for the Degar people, the indigenous inhabitants of Vietnam's Central Highlands. The main tribes, in order of population, are the Jarai, Rhade, Bahnar, Koho, Mnong, and Stieng. Recruited heavily by U.S. Special Forces operating in the tri-border region, their loyalty and bravery earned the enduring respect and affection of the Americans.

Nung—Minority group of ethnic Chinese living in Vietnam. Loyal soldiers and fierce fighters who played a variety of roles with U.S. Army Special Forces, including that of recon team members.

NVA—North Vietnamese Army regulars; the North Vietnam Communist element.

One-Zero—Designation for a SOG team leader. The assistant team leader was the **One-One** and the radio man was the **One-Two**.

Over the Fence (Across the Fence, Over the Wire, Across the Wire)—Operating beyond the Vietnamese border in Laos or Cambodia.

Prairie Fire—Code name for cross-border missions into Laos.

Prairie Fire Emergency—Term to designate a team in contact with the enemy and requiring immediate extraction.

PRC-25—Field radio carried by recon teams and support elements to communicate with FACs or FOBs; aka "Prick" 25.

Recon Team (RT)—See **Spike Team**.

RON—Remain Overnight. Generally used to describe a recon team's sleeping area at night.

RPG (rocket-propelled grenade.)—Russian designed shoulder-fired weapon system utilized by the NVA. Consists of launcher with warhead affixed to and propelled by a fin-stabilized rocket motor.

RT-10—Small emergency survival radio carried by U.S. personnel on recon teams. Put out a signal to attract aircraft and provided voice communication when the aircraft got close enough.

SFOB—Special Forces Operating Base. Generally used to describe the 5th SFG headquarters in Nha Trang.

SLAM (Search, Locate, Annihilate, Monitor) Company—A company-sized unit, less a weapons platoon, that was used to reinforce recon teams or attack suitable targets found by the recon teams.

Sledgehammer—Radio Relay/Signal Intercept site located near Co Groc Mountain on Hill 1438 in Kontum Province at coordinates YA806695. Established to provide commo link between RTs in Cambodia and FOB2. Manned by FOB2 Hatchet Platoon and a few 4th Division personnel. Closed in March 1969 and replaced with Klondike.

Slick—Passenger-carrying helicopters; either Bell UH-1 Hueys flown by U.S. pilots, or Sikorsky CH-34 "Kingbees" flown by Vietnamese pilots.

Snake—Code name for Cobra helicopter gunships.

Soap Bubble—Code name for indigenous personnel on a recon team.

SPAD—Air Force A1-E or A1-H single-engine fighter aircraft used in support of SOG operations.

SPAF—"Sneaky Pete Air Force." Army O-1 Bird Dog pilots who served as forward air controllers supporting SOG missions.

Spare 39er—Request for extraction by a recon team.

Spike Team (ST)—Nine-to-twelve-member teams used by SOG to run reconnaissance missions in Laos, Cambodia, and the DMZ. Teams were made up of U.S. and indigenous personnel. Designation changed to Recon Team (RT) in summer 1968.

Spooky Gunship—C-47 aircraft with mini-guns mounted onboard to supply close support to ground troops in Vietnam.

Straw Hat—Code name for American personnel on a recon team.

Strings—120-foot ropes on the helicopters for rappel-in insertions or McGuire rig extractions.

Swedish K—9mm submachine gun; often fitted with silencers and used by some recon team members.

Swiss Seat—12-foot lengths of rappelling rope carried by all recon team members, which could be tied around the waist and legs to form a seat that could be snap-linked to the strings on a helicopter for insertion or extraction.

TNT—Trinitrotoluene, a highly explosive material.

Toe Popper—Small antipersonnel mines used by recon teams to deter trackers; they were designed to blow off a foot but not kill. By badly injuring the victim rather than killing him, trackers operating in pairs would be deterred when one had to stay with his comrade to care for him.

Turtle—Code name used by chase medics and Covey to describe slicks (passenger carrying helicopters).

URC-10—Small emergency survival radio carried by each U.S. member of a recon team. Was later replaced by the RT-10 version.

VC—Vietcong, the South Vietnamese Communist faction.

Xe Xou—River in Laos that cuts through the FOB2/CCC area of operations. Its meanderings created the landmark named the Bra near the junction of Highway 110 and Highway 96 in southern Laos. *Xe* is the Laotian designation for river. The Vietnamese would refer to this river as the Dak Xou.

'Yard camp—Located on Route 14 approximately five kilometers south of FOB2 at Coordinates AR766814. Originally built in 1967 to keep Montagnard Hatchet Force personnel separated from Vietnamese and Nungs.

Introduction

My Reasons for Enlisting in the U.S. Army—April 1966

The team split up where the trail divided into several paths that wound into the dense brush in front of us. I was ever so silently proceeding down the left path. As I rounded a turn that skirted a large bush, the dreaded whispered sound broke the silence.

"Bang-bang, you're dead."

It was a neighbor, David Dopkant, a member of the opposing force, who had shot me. I was six years old and playing commandos near my home in Gardner, Massachusetts. I turned and silently made my way back to the starting point, a ground level area of exposed ledge where our games began. We would divide up into opposing sides and take turns being the side that would hide and then the side whose job it was to search the other one out. The first to see his opponent would announce his "kill" with a "Bang-bang, you're dead." My peers ranged from my age to three years older. David Dopkant was one of the older boys. His father served in the Army in World War II and had fought and was wounded in the Battle of the Bulge.

As I reluctantly walked back to the starting area, two things burned their way into my memory. First, it occurred to me that if this were real war, the "bang-bang" that had killed me would have been loud and alerted my teammates. Second, I realized I would be dead. The very thought of this puzzled, confounded, and frightened me. I could not begin to comprehend what dying would be like. It was at that moment I began to understand that men who played the game for real must be exceedingly brave to put everything on the line and walk down the path to combat.

From then on, David's father had my utmost respect because I knew that he was one of these men.

Little did I know that 19 years later I would have the opportunity to walk down the same path. Only then did I become aware, with the introduction to things like silenced weapons, how startlingly real and true to life were our childhood games.

◊ ◊ ◊

In early 1966 American involvement in the Vietnam War was increasing dramatically. As a junior at the University of Massachusetts, I engaged in many a discussion—in the classroom, on campus, and at the local watering holes—regarding the justification of U.S. participation in the conflict. During those years of my life, I had been deeply influenced by President John F. Kennedy's views and philosophy. I found it incomprehensible that the majority of my fellow students either were not listening to his speeches or were too self-centered to care about anything else. When he said, "Ask not what your country can do for you; ask what you can do for your country;" or "We shall … support any friend, oppose any foe, in order to assure the survival and success of liberty;" most students viewed this as rhetoric designed to make suckers of the American people. To me it was obvious that my generation was one of spoiled brats who were outraged that they might get drafted should they flunk out of school.

At that time and to this day, I define that as cowardice by a generation who had fathers and grandfathers who fought two world wars so that their children would not have to go through what they went through. The majority opinion was "it is my right," with little thought of responsibilities and obligations as members of American society.

Individual rights were the major concern of the left-wing liberal academics, both students and teachers. It was these same liberals who would deny others their rights with one-sided interpretations of the U.S. Constitution. After my return to UMass following my tour of duty in Vietnam, a well-known cabinet member of the government was scheduled to speak there about the war. The students attending booed and jeered so loudly that the speech was cancelled. The students seemed to feel that their freedom of speech was sacred, but that of others was not. The faculty brought their anti-war bias into the classroom, and it was the far wiser student who reflected the political dogma of his professor in his writings. In actuality, students were then and still are today deprived of their constitutional right to free speech by teachers with political ideologies who espouse them in the classroom. Who would dare take a contrary stance to the professor's if one's grade might suffer?

There was no single explanation for why I disassociated myself from academia and enlisted in the U.S. Army. The reasons ranged from having my bluff called following discussions concerning the Vietnam War to a curiosity about combat fostered as a youth playing commandos. More than once I was told, as a result of my support of American involvement, that "If you feel that strongly, why don't you join the military and go and fight?" Other reasons were that I agreed with the belief that one has an obligation to one's country and that I desired to put some discipline in my life. The student role had become a bore, but I really didn't know what I wanted to do next. The thought of adding some excitement to my existence seemed appealing, and I would also be fulfilling my obligation to my country for the wonderful lifestyle I and other Americans were enjoying.

But the primary reason I enlisted was due to the strong impression made on me by John F. Kennedy. Military service during the Vietnam War represented my way of "asking what I could do for my country." I have always felt, and still feel, that the Vietnam War was a just cause in the fight against Communist expansion in that country and an honorable and noble effort by the United States to defend freedom in the world.

My apologies to those who do not like "I" stories. I feel I can only comment on experiences that I had and try to make it clear when I am relating my interpretations of the actions and reasoning of others. Individuals in combat situations perceive things differently because they view events from different perspectives. In the "fog of war," simply occupying the wrong spot on the battlefield can mean the difference between life and death. Sometimes the reasoning of individuals is in synch with their comrades and sometimes it is not. This adds to the confusion of battle and makes heroes of some and cowards of others.

This book is not intended to be a chronicle of heroes and cowards, but of my observations and memories of events presented in as accurate and unembellished a manner as possible. My reason for writing it is to provide what insights I had as a witness to the actions of some truly outstanding men. The incidents depicted were compiled from notes, firsthand accounts, and recollections jotted down over the course of 50 years.

Meeting with ex-SOG members at the annual Special Operations Association Reunion (SOAR) over the years jogged my thoughts countless times and brought many faded memories back into sharp focus. In talking to individuals who had lost loved ones nearly 40 years before, I came to realize the majority had a great interest in the most minute details of the circumstances surrounding the loss of their family members. I have tried, to the best of my ability, to present what I saw and to make it clear when my statements are the result of information passed to me.

The attempt to reassemble the complete stories of what happened so long ago can only be done by collecting the thoughts and comments of those who witnessed or were a part of the events. Of course, the complete stories can never be wholly reassembled because we will never have the insights of the dead and missing.

Joseph F. Parnar
RA11960075
August 12, 1966, to April 14, 1969

CHAPTER I

Airborne Infantry

During the spring of 1966, I was a junior at the University of Massachusetts, majoring in physical education. But U.S involvement in Vietnam was gearing up and I wanted to see what it was like to fight in a war and how I would acquit myself. I left school in April 1966 and saw my local recruiter, who arranged testing and a physical exam in early May. I passed the physical and mental tests and was advised that with my scores, I could request any field open in the Army at that time. I requested Airborne Infantry. The recruiter was quite surprised at my choice. The reason I selected Airborne Infantry was because a friend from where I worked during the summer, Mr. Henry Zablonski, someone whom I respected and who had himself been in the military, told me, "Go Airborne—those guys are tough." Also, one of my mother's cousins had served in the airborne in World War II and received a Purple Heart for wounds received in action. Our family was quite proud of his service.

I enlisted in the United States Army for Airborne Infantry and arranged with the recruiter to start in August. I figured this would give me three months to party and have my last hurrah before committing to three years of service. But because my student status ended when I withdrew from UMass, I was called up for a draft physical in June. To my surprise, a couple of weeks later I received a letter telling me I was medically disqualified and would be retested in one month. I was retested in July and the only thing I needed to have done again was my chest X-ray. I hitchhiked back from Boston with a friend from the neighboring town of

Templeton, John Gemborys, who like me had decided to enlist. He had chosen the Marine Corps. When I was discharged from the service almost three years later, I would learn that John had been killed in Vietnam.

On August 12, 1966, I was sworn in at the induction center at Springfield, Massachusetts. I was immediately sent for basic training at Fort Dix in New Jersey from August to October. Having been a junior at the University of Massachusetts and a member of the varsity gymnastics team, I found basic to be easy both mentally and physically. I also found it to be something that for the first time in my life was relevant, important, and meaningful.

While I was at Fort Dix, my mother forwarded another letter I had received from the local draft board. The result was still "medically disqualified, retest in one month." I tore this letter into small pieces and flushed it down the toilet in our barracks. I was afraid that if my drill sergeant, Sergeant DeMule, found it, I might get kicked out of the Army.

In her accompanying letter, my mother wrote to inform me that my closest friend from Gardner, Alan Virta, had been drafted into the Army about two weeks after I went to Springfield to be sworn in. Al and I had gone barhopping the night before I left, and he made a point of telling me repeatedly he would take care of all the available women in the Gardner area in my absence. I really got a chuckle out of the fact that he was now in the service like me. Al never voiced support for the war in Vietnam like I had, but I gained lifelong respect for him for entering the military and not running to Canada, as some others chose to do. Al beat me to Vietnam too, arriving almost a year before I did and serving his tour with the 1st Infantry Division— "The Big Red One." Even though we only see each other occasionally since he now resides in Kentucky, I still consider Al one of my closest friends.

I was never one to write letters very often and had been in the Army around four weeks before communicating with my parents. They did not have a telephone at the time I entered the service, so calling home was not an option. In the same letter mentioned above, my mom chewed me out for not writing to tell them where I was. I immediately wrote and started my reply with, "We just got back from the field …." Somehow, I figured this white lie would take some of the sting out of my inconsiderateness. This ploy would be repeated in most of my letters home for the next three years as my excuse for procrastinating.

After basic, I was sent to Fort Gordon, Georgia, for advanced individual training (AIT) geared to Airborne Infantry. Again, I found the training to be meaningful and relevant. It was at Fort Gordon that I made friends with Pvt. Tom Deschenes, who bunked next to me. We hit it off immediately as he was from Fitchburg, Massachusetts and also had attended UMass. After I was discharged from active military service, I learned that Tom was killed in Vietnam in June 1967 while serving with the 173rd Airborne Brigade.

At Fort Gordon a Special Forces recruiter gave a presentation and I found my name on the list of those qualified to take the entry tests. My friend Tom Deschenes wanted to try for Special Forces very much, but part of the requirement was that applicants must be 20 years old and Tom was just shy of that. I passed the test and volunteered for Special Forces. A major reason for my volunteering was because President John F. Kennedy had spoken highly of this elite unit and authorized the wearing of the Green Beret as the official headgear of Special Forces. After my AIT was complete, I went home for Christmas leave in December 1966.

After Christmas leave, I reported to Fort Benning, Georgia for jump school. Once again, Tom Deschenes and I went through together. We were in the same platoon with a Navy SEAL Underwater Demolitions Team (UDT) that was also going through the course. They trained as a team, and I was very impressed by their physical fitness and their esprit de corps. Until then I had never been aware of the inter-service rivalry that existed between the Navy and the Marines. According to these fellows, the word Marine stood for "My Ass Rides In Navy Equipment." They also had a humorous rhyme they liked to repeat:

> Leathernecks on bended knees
> Can kiss the ass of UDTs.
> Although they say they're first ashore
> UDTs were there before.

They took over leadership of our barracks for the next three weeks and got everyone organized and we never failed an inspection. After that, I always had the greatest respect for the Navy SEALs.

We completed parachute training at the end of January 1967, and
Tom and I parted ways when he reported to his airborne unit. Those
of us who were accepted for Special Forces training were held over at
Fort Benning for a couple of extra days. During this time, I got to meet
one of the other people whom I would be training with for the next
11 months.

Mike Deason was from Macon, Georgia, and, like me, a college
dropout. I believe he had played freshman football at the University of
Georgia. He was a big man, standing 6′3″ or 6′4″ and weighing about
240. When I first met him, he had accidentally slashed his thigh with
a banana knife while cutting down his basic training combat boots to
make them into a pair of low quarters. Unlike me, Mike already knew
he wanted to be a medic in Special Forces. He proceeded to stitch up
the wound with a straight needle and thread, using aftershave lotion as
an antiseptic, with no local anesthetic. I wondered if all Special Forces
applicants were expected to be this tough, as I didn't think I could have
sewed myself up like Mike had.

After the two days waiting, we were bused to Fort Bragg, North
Carolina and arrived at mid-afternoon on a Saturday.

CHAPTER 2

Special Forces Training—Medic

When I first reported to Fort Bragg, we were required to choose a specialty from those required by the Special Forces A Team. These included organization and intelligence, weapons, communications, engineering, and medical—the last three being the only specialties open to personnel on their first enlistment. My initial inclination was for engineering, which included demolitions training, but my adviser said that with all the anatomy and physiology courses I had taken while attending the University of Massachusetts as a physical education major, medical would be a natural fit for me. This, plus the fact that a medical class was about to start, while there would be an eight-week wait for the next engineering class with KP (kitchen patrol) every other day, led me to agree to it. Medic training was the longest of all the specialties, lasting 37 weeks.

The first part of our training was four weeks of field exercises with particular emphasis on map reading, land navigation, patrolling, ambushes, reconnaissance, and general field maneuvers. Upon completion of this phase, we were issued Green Berets. We were not, however, permitted to have a group flash sewn on them as that privilege was reserved only for those who had successfully completed their specialty training. We pinned our Special Forces crest to the beret in the area where the flash would have been sewn on. This made sure that everyone knew that we were only Training Group trainees and not Special Forces qualified. After this, we got into the specific medical instruction.

It began with an eight-week course at Fort Bragg in medical terminology and anatomy. Immediately, I found that Special Forces training differed from anything I had experienced in basic, AIT, or jump school. There were eight hours of classes five days a week, and a test at the end of each week. I found the classes to be as difficult as, or even more difficult than, most of my classes at UMass, including those when I was a chemistry major. The primary difference was that these classes had a much higher degree of relevancy to what we were being trained for.

Another significant thing that stood out when we began Special Forces training was that the harassment, ever present in basic, AIT, and jump school, eased considerably. We still had an inspection every Saturday that determined whether we got the weekend off and were still assigned work details when not attending classes. The inspections were made easier because our barracks were all brand new and easy to keep clean. Of my class of medics, I would estimate 80 to 90 percent had some college experience behind them. Some, like Bob Armstrong, had already received his B.S. and was a qualified teacher.

Many others had played football in college, and this contributed to the success of the excellent flag football team our class fielded the fall of 1967. Some of the participants had freshman football experience at schools like Oklahoma, Georgia, UCLA, and other such football factories. Our flag football team was runner-up for the Fort Bragg championship despite injuries to our star running back. I steered clear of football myself, as I only weighed around 155 and figured I would get killed playing against people weighing 200 to 240 pounds.

After our daily classes—and if we passed our Saturday morning inspection—we were free to go to town and do what we wanted in our time off. For most of us, this meant barhopping in Fayetteville. The two individuals with whom I became closest were Ron Jungling and Jerry Krizan. Ron was from Oklahoma and had attended Oklahoma Military Academy, so he was quite familiar with military protocol. Jerry was from Muskegon, Michigan, and one weekend he flew home and returned with his mother's car, which provided us with many rides into Fayetteville during our time off. Our partying in town was curtailed to a great extent by the limited funds available to us, as we were all only making between $110 and $130 per month depending on our rank and pay grade.

One of our classmates, Fred Holdsworth, had served in the Peace Corps and had pictures of himself at the graduation ceremony of the first class

Class 68-3 members in medical whites (L–R): Michael Randall, Chuck Willoughby, Ron Jungling, Angelo Holt, James Van. (Bryon Loucks photo)

of Peace Corps volunteers on the White House lawn with President Kennedy. He served his tour in Gabon, Africa and met Albert Schweitzer while in service there. I found his stories about his experiences fascinating.

Next was the 10-week Special Forces Medical Training Course at Fort Sam Houston in San Antonio, Texas. These classes were among the most difficult of the Special Forces Medic curriculum, and nearly all of them were taught by MDs. Working on each other or with dummies, we learned many of the fundamental medical procedures such as suturing; taking blood pressure, pulse, and temperature; administering mouth-to-mouth resuscitation and external heart massage; giving inoculations and vaccinations; inserting gastric and nasal tubes. We practiced cricothyroidotomies (cutting emergency airways) on live goats, did catheterizations on dummies, and studied anatomy on cadavers.

The course also covered the essentials of medical diagnosis and treatment. When we attended classes at Fort Sam, we did not wear regular OD Army fatigues, but were issued white uniforms. We were permitted to wear our Green Berets with the whites however. We graduated in July 1967 as Special Forces Medical Class 68-3. We were now full-fledged Army medics.

It was around this time that my first flare-up of eczema occurred. It started with what I thought was an insect bite on my right forearm. I guess I must have scratched at it, as it never properly healed. It was like a quarter-sized patch that resembled a floor burn that would not scab over but instead would encrust with dried body fluid. When I would take a shower, the patch would dissolve and begin weeping body fluid anew. This condition would remain with me into my tour in Vietnam a year later. I never went on sick call for the patch because it might have caused me to miss some of my critical medical training with the possibility of being recycled and not graduating with my class.

Our next phase of training was on-the-job training (OJT). Six of my classmates and I were sent to work at the Ireland Army Hospital at Fort Knox, Kentucky. The rest of our classmates were dispersed to various Army hospitals throughout the United States. During this phase we would spend part of our days assigned to an MD and accompany him on his rounds. We also spent part of the day working in various wards such as intensive care, the emergency room, pediatrics, dependents' clinic, and various others. We got to scrub in and observe two appendectomies in surgery. Once again, the training was intensive, applicable, and relevant.

When we first got to Fort Knox, we were issued new I.D. cards that had a medic cross superimposed over the face, thus classifying us as Army medics. Ironically, these cards were taken away as soon as we got back to Fort Bragg, where we were issued new ones that changed our designation from medic to "aide man." I believe this was done because regular medics were only permitted to carry a .45-caliber pistol for defensive purposes, while a Special Forces medic was also a soldier who had a need to carry offensive weapons.

After our seven weeks of OJT, our class reassembled at Fort Bragg for a six-week course in diagnosis and treatment of tropical diseases. MDs again taught the majority of the classes. After tropical diseases, we entered the final course in surgery called "Dog Lab." Each of us was issued a dog to serve as our patient. Mine was a mixed-breed female that resembled a small greyhound with long, tapered legs and stood about 20 inches tall. She had a mostly black and dark brown coat with some white on her belly. Though we weren't really supposed to, I sometimes would buy canned dog food and bring it to her as a treat.

For the next four weeks, we maintained charts on our patients—recording pulse, respiration, and rectal temperature. During this time, we did fecal and urine analysis and blood work in the lab to determine our patients' ability to withstand surgery. Following the four-week period, a gun-shot wound was inflicted to the fleshy part of the rear thigh while the dogs were under anesthesia. We took them into surgery, debrided the wound, dressed it, and left it open to granulate in from the bottom as one would do for ordinary combat wounds. The next day I went to the kennel to check on my patient. The ace bandage that I had used to cover the surgical dressings had come unwrapped and was now trailing behind her as she excitedly began climbing over the other dogs in her cage to get closer to me. I wondered how this dog could feel such affection for me after what had been done to her.

For the next couple of weeks, we nursed our patients back to health before taking them back into surgery, where we closed their wounds. At this point we performed amputations of the two front paws and terminated our patients with a 50 percent solution of sodium pentothal injected directly into the heart. We each played all parts of the surgical team, serving as surgeon, assistant surgeon, anesthesiologist, and instrument passer.

I found this portion of our training to be most trying, as I love animals and felt terrible in performing the procedures on one that had put her complete trust in me. For a while I was even thinking of how I might smuggle my dog off the base and put her on a bus to Gardner where my parents could pick her up. Eventually, I realized you can't buy a bus ticket for a dog and it would also have meant the immediate end of my Medic and Special Forces training. The only thing that enabled me to complete the training was that I believed the experience might someday help me save the life of another human being.

Once during Dog Lab, a sergeant was demonstrating how to deal with morphine poisoning. A dog was brought in and given an overdose by an injection. A few minutes later the sergeant administered a dose of nalorphine, which was supposed to counter the effects of the morphine. Except this time, it didn't work. Either the dosage was not correct or he had waited too long. The dog did not wake up. Someone in the room stifled a laugh when it became clear what had happened. The sergeant looked up angrily and ordered us to "never laugh at death." Another

Special Forces Medical Class 68-3—Fort Sam Houston, San Antonio, Texas, July 1967. (Bryon Loucks photo)

dog was brought in, and the demonstration was repeated. This time the dog awoke following the second injection.

After Dog Lab we were finished with our medical studies and went before the review board for a final testing. The review board consisted of six MD's and one sergeant who quizzed us on all aspects of our training. After passing the review board, we entered a final phase called Phase IV, or what is now known as "Robin Sage." It consisted of classroom instruction in guerrilla warfare and a field exercise in the pinelands south of Fayetteville near Camp Mackall that culminated in a 30-mile hike with full rucksacks. This completed our training and qualified us as full-fledged Green Berets. We were now permitted to wear the full flash of the unit to which we would be assigned.

CHAPTER 3

Vietnam Assignment

Upon completion of our training, we submitted an application for preference of duty assignments. We were allowed to request three assignments. Everyone in my graduating class of 44 medics asked for Vietnam on all three choices. Some requested specific Corps areas of Vietnam such as I Corps, II Corps, III Corps, IV Corps, or some combination thereof. When our orders came down, not one of us got orders for Vietnam.

I, along with many of my friends, was assigned to the 7th SFG (Special Forces Group) at Fort Bragg. Others were assigned to the 3rd and 6th SFG at Fort Bragg. A few were to be sent to language school in California, a few to Germany, Panama, or Okinawa. We were all deeply disappointed. I was beginning to think that I would never get to Vietnam since I was now approaching the halfway point in my three-year enlistment. I figured if I spent one year with the 7th, it would not give me the necessary full year's time remaining in service to get to Vietnam. And my primary reason for enlisting was specifically to go to Vietnam.

After graduation, we all went home for leave in December 1967. One of my medical class fellow graduates, Chuck Willoughby, offered me a ride to Washington, D.C., from where I would fly home to Massachusetts. Chuck was the nephew of Congressman Alphonso E. Bell, Jr. from California, and he had his uncle's car, having visited him the weekend before our graduation. It was quite a ride. The car had Congressional plates on it, and Chuck averaged around 90 mph on the trip up Route 95 to D.C. On one occasion we had a Highway Patrol car pull up about

Mrs. Billye Alexander. (Reprinted with permission from *The Green Beret Magazine*, Radix Press, www.specialforcesbooks.com)

six feet behind our rear bumper, but he backed off when he saw the Congressional plates.

During our training, we had often heard of a woman who worked at the Pentagon named Mrs. Billye Alexander (also referred to as "Mrs. A."), who was supposedly in charge of all overseas replacements for Special Forces. On our trip I asked Chuck to drop me off at the Pentagon building because I intended to seek out Mrs. Alexander and get on the manifest for Vietnam. When he dropped me off, he handed me his uncle's business card and told me to call him at the number printed on the card if I got anywhere in my quest.

As I approached the building, I began to doubt whether my idea was such a good one after all. I never knew the Pentagon was so huge, and I didn't see any signs indicating a main entrance. I proceeded up a walkway that led to what looked like a loading dock with a uniformed guard standing on the platform. I was in uniform at the time and the guard asked, "Can I help you, specialist?"

I replied, "Yes, sir, I'm looking for Mrs. Alexander."

He said to me, "She's on the sixth corridor, C ring. If you go through this door, it will put you on the E ring. Go down until you get to the sixth corridor and go in two more rings. Ask someone in that area for directions." I didn't realize it at the time, but it was somewhat of a miracle that he had even heard of Mrs. Alexander since approximately 15,000 people worked in the Pentagon at that time.

I entered the building as instructed, but when I got to the junction of the sixth corridor and the C ring, there was no clerk or guard to provide further instructions. I was standing there looking puzzled when an Army major stopped and inquired, "Can I help you, specialist?"

I again replied, "Yes, sir, I'm looking for Mrs. Alexander."

He pointed down a side hallway off the sixth corridor and said, "Go down that hallway and ask someone; she works in that area."

A short distance down the hallway, the space opened into a huge office room with perhaps a hundred desks with people working at them. I didn't see anything that resembled a receptionist and was once again standing and looking puzzled. A WAC (Women's Army Corps) major approached and asked if she could help me. For the third time, I gave the response that had worked so well to get me to this point.

She replied, "See the blonde woman working at the desk five rows in and two desks over? That's her."

"Do I need an appointment to see her?"

"No, you can go right there."

I zigzagged between the desks, approached hers, and introduced myself. I told Mrs. Alexander that I had heard that she was in charge of Special Forces overseas replacements and I wanted to get on the manifest to go to Vietnam. She took my name, rank, and serial number and directed me to a waiting room that said "E-7 and Above" while she had someone pull my records.

When I entered the waiting room, a sergeant major was seated there reading a magazine. Up to that point in my military career, I had practically no exposure to sergeant majors and figured they ate Pfc.s and

Sp4c.s for breakfast. I grabbed a copy of *Time* magazine and pretended to read it. He piped up, "Specialist, I think the enlisted men's waiting room is the next one down."

"Mrs. Alexander told me to come in here and wait," I replied.

His response to this was, "Oh."

A few minutes later a WAC private entered the waiting room and said, "Specialist Parnar, Mrs. Alexander will see you now."

It was my moment of glory in the military. I said to the sergeant major, "Take it easy, sergeant major. We'll see ya." I later found out that Mrs. Alexander also was responsible for all overseas replacements for E-7 and above. Apparently, the sergeant major had been waiting to see her too.

When I talked to Mrs. Alexander, she explained that the 5th Special Forces personnel were not turning over until April 1968. I inquired about the 46th Company in Thailand, a unit that I learned of while at Bragg that had conducted some missions related to the war in Vietnam, but she said they were not turning over until August 1968. I asked her to please put me on the manifest for Vietnam in April. It was then she said, "We have openings for SOG in April. Do you know much about SOG?"

I replied that I did and asked to be put on the manifest for SOG. In actuality, I had only heard of SOG, the name being an acronym for Studies and Observations Group, and the only thing anyone ever said concerning it was that SOG was the hairiest assignment in Vietnam. The rumor was that everyone either got killed or wounded. No one at Bragg who knew of or had served with SOG ever talked about it and denied any knowledge of the unit or its missions. After I thanked Mrs. Alexander again for helping me, she said she preferred sending people to Vietnam who wanted to go rather than those who did not. I was a little shaky as I made my way out of the Pentagon, not sure what I had just volunteered for.

When I got to the street, I went to a phone booth near where Willoughby had dropped me off and called the number on his uncle's card. Chuck answered and I informed him I was on the manifest for SOG for April. He asked where I was and I told him a phone booth just down the street from where he had left me. He said for me to stay right there, and after 10 minutes he pulled up. Chuck asked where I had gone in and I told him to go up the walkway toward the loading dock. He said to wait in his uncle's car in a No Parking zone, while he went inside to attempt to repeat my actions. I guess the Congressional plates on the car worked as no one bothered me while I sat there. When he returned, Willoughby was also on the manifest for SOG in April. He then gave me a ride to the airport.

CHAPTER 4

7th SFG, Vietnam, and MACV-SOG

When I reported to the 7th SFG in January 1968, I was told that the paperwork for my "secret" security clearance was not in my files and I would have to re-apply. I was a bit concerned about the effect this would have on my orders for Vietnam in April, since this clearance was necessary to be fully Special Forces qualified. In the meantime, I had to wear a small red bar on my beret in place of the full red 7th SFG flash.

I was assigned to work in the 7th SFG dispensary while I waited for my orders to come down. Starting in February, I began going to the orderly room of the 7th to check to see if my orders were there yet. After a week or so, the NCOIC (non-commissioned officer in charge) asked me, "What makes you think you're getting orders for Vietnam?"

I replied I had seen Mrs. Alexander in December and I was to be on the manifest for April deployment to Vietnam. I got read the riot act and was told I wasn't supposed to see Mrs. Alexander and should have requested a transfer through official paperwork.

My orders finally did come down toward the end of February, and I went home for a 30-day leave prior to departing for Vietnam at the beginning of April.

◊ ◊ ◊

I reported to Fort Lewis, Washington, in early April and was processed for transfer to Vietnam. I was among a group that flew over on a Flying Tiger commercial airliner with a one-hour stop in Anchorage, Alaska and a two-hour stop at an air base in Japan for refueling. With us were a good number of medics from my graduating class who had called Mrs.

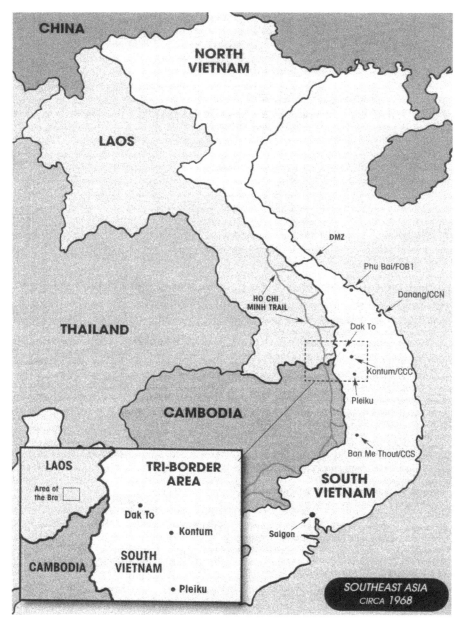

Southeast Asia circa 1968. (From original edition of *SOG Medic* by Paladin Press)

Alexander after Willoughby and I spread the word that Mrs. "A" really did exist and could get you to Vietnam.

We landed at the base at Cam Ranh Bay for in-country processing. On the flight, my eczema flared up again, probably due to the reduced air pressure in the plane. Numerous weeping patches broke out on my legs and waist. It was very annoying because the dried body fluids stuck to my khaki uniform and left discolored stains. I tried using small pieces of toilet paper to cover the patches such as one does after nicking oneself while shaving, but it didn't do much good. The flight took about 22 hours and we were in the plane for more than a day with the stopovers, making it a very uncomfortable trip for me.

After preliminary in-processing in Cam Ranh Bay, we were trucked to the 5th Special Forces Headquarters in Nha Trang for further in-processing. At the 5th Group Headquarters, I was advised that my secret security clearance had not caught up with me yet, so I was assigned to work in the transient barracks arms room on a 24-hours on, 24-hours off basis. I needed the full secret security clearance in my file before an interim top secret clearance could be issued permitting me to go to SOG.

During one of my 24-hours off shifts, I went to the beach in Nha Trang hoping the sun exposure would have a healing effect on my eczema. Instead I got badly sunburned. This, in addition to my flaring eczema, caused my entire chest to become one huge scab. I also had a touch of sun poisoning. I went to the 5th Group dispensary and they put me on a helicopter and flew me to Cam Ranh Bay to the dermatology clinic. When I arrived, I was told that they would keep me there over the weekend and if I didn't get better, I would be sent back to the States. This really panicked me because I didn't enlist in the Army to avoid Vietnam. I explained that I had duty in Nha Trang and needed to go back there. The doctor at the clinic had prescribed Burroughs solution soaks for my condition. I told him that since I was a medic, I would treat myself and if my condition did not improve would report back the following week.

At first my condition did not improve—if anything, it worsened. Small water blisters erupted around my fingernail beds and got infected, but I was able to control them with erythromycin that I got from the 5th Group dispensary. I never went back to the dermatology clinic.

◊ ◊ ◊

One night while I was working in the transient barracks arms room at Nha Trang, some mortar rounds were fired into the compound, and it was then that I learned a lesson that would benefit me later in my tour. At night, mortar positions on the 5th Group compound would periodically fire off illumination rounds, and at first I could not tell the difference between the sound of incoming and outgoing rounds. Then I noticed that because nearly all of the military-built buildings in Vietnam had roofs made of corrugated metal sheets, after incoming rounds you could always hear the sound of the sand sprinkling down on the metal roofs.

◊ ◊ ◊

After nearly a month in Nha Trang, my full secret security clearance arrived. I was issued an interim top secret clearance and flown to Da Nang for processing into SOG along with other Special Forces personnel. During in-processing, we were given a briefing by a major in which we learned more about the nature of SOG's activities—running reconnaissance missions along the Ho Chi Minh Trail in Laos and Cambodia.

The major emphasized that these missions were classified "Top Secret, Limdis (Limited Distribution), never to be declassified or downgraded." He told us the missions were run by reconnaissance teams, also termed Spike Teams, made up of three Americans and up to nine indigenous personnel—usually Vietnamese, Chinese Nungs, or Montagnards. (The designation Spike Team would later be changed to Recon Team.) The team leader was designated the One-Zero, the assistant team leader the One-One, and the radio man the One-Two. At CCN (Command and Control North), at FOB1 (Forward Operations Base One) in Phu Bai, the Spike Teams were generally named after snakes; at FOB2 in Kontum, the names of states of the United States were used; and at FOB5 in Ban Me Thout, it was the names of tools.

There were also platoon-sized elements to support the recon teams called Hatchet Platoons, and company-sized elements called SLAM (Search, Locate, Annihilate, Monitor) Companies. These units could come to the aid of Spike Teams or attack other suitable targets discovered by the recon teams.

MACV-SOG (Military Assistance Command Vietnam—Studies and Observations Group), was not part of the regular military command structure in Vietnam, and our boss, called "Chief SOG," reported directly to Washington, D.C. SOG was a joint service command with personnel from the Army, Navy, Air Force and Marines, and involved several different groups. I was assigned to SOG's OP-35 (Ground Studies Group), which was made up mostly of Army Special Forces personnel filtered to SOG through the 5th Special Forces Group's Special Operations Augmentation. The major instructed us not to keep diaries or journals and not to discuss our missions or the unit with anyone not assigned to SOG. He said to tell our relatives at home we were "training Montagnards" as our cover story. I was issued the code name "Transistor" and learned that I would be assigned to FOB2 in Kontum Province, where SOG operated in the tri-border area of Vietnam, southern Laos, and northern Cambodia.

Missions into Laos had been given the code designation "Prairie Fire," and those into Cambodia carried the code name "Daniel Boone." When a team came into enemy contact and was in danger of being overrun, it could declare a "Prairie Fire emergency," which had exceedingly high priority; any aircraft flying in Vietnam at that time could be diverted for support. Spike Teams served "Bright Light" duty, which was the emergency rescue of downed pilots in Laos, Cambodia, or North Vietnam. Bright Light was also used to designate those operations that involved going to the assistance of other Spike Teams or trying to find missing team members.

Among the missions conducted by the Spike Teams were reconnaissance of specified target areas; road watches, which involved counting the number and type of enemy trucks traveling down the trail; bomb damage assessments following air strikes; the implanting of sensors and wiretaps and other monitoring devices; ambushes of enemy units; destruction of enemy caches; and occasionally the snatching of enemy prisoners.

Spike Teams also planted booby-trapped enemy ammunition in enemy caches and along trails. This consisted of spiked AK-47 ammo and doctored mortar rounds. This ordnance was referred to by the code names "Eldest Son" or "Italian Green." The booby-trapped ammo was designed to blow the bolt out of an AK-47 or explode in a mortar tube, causing injury or death to those using them. It was supposed to make the enemy become wary and learn to distrust their weapons systems.

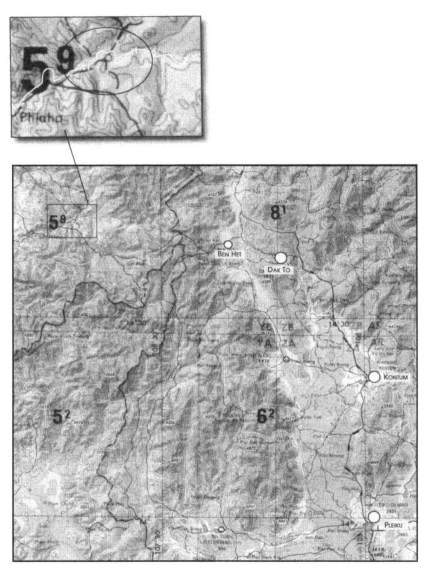

The map above shows the FOB2/CCC area of operations where missions were launched during the author's tour of duty (May 1968 to April 1969). Missions were conducted up to a depth of 20 miles into Laos and Cambodia. The white dots indicate the major cities in the Central Highlands—Ben Het, Dak To, Kontum, and Pleiku—and their relationship to the tri-border area. The close up above-left shows the landmark known as the "Bra," a double curve of the Xe Xou River. (From original edition of *SOG Medic* by Paladin Press)

The major informed us that at the FOBs, SOG officers were not to be saluted. This was because SOG did not operate like traditional military units. It was a meritocracy, with proven experience being the criteria for determining who was in charge. It was not uncommon for a second or first lieutenant, even a captain, to report to a staff sergeant, sergeant, specialist fourth class, or a private first class during the course of a mission. For the most part, only those who had demonstrated their abilities in the field were made recon One-Zeros.

After the major finished his briefing, we were addressed by a colonel. The first thing he told us was "You men will be running some of the most important missions in Vietnam. Someday books will be written about what you men will be doing." My initial thought was "What about what the major had said?" Who was going to be writing these books if our operations were "never to be declassified?" I said nothing, however. I had already learned from my previous training that it didn't pay to be logical or a wise guy in the U.S. Army, even in Special Forces.

The colonel also warned us never to piss off pilots because it was they who would be bringing us our beer, movies, and entertainment as well as pulling our asses out of hot spots in the boonies. He strongly suggested that it was our duty to buy pilots a drink whenever they came in our clubs at the FOB. He was sure right about that.

Finally, we were informed that anyone present who wanted out of their SOG assignment was welcome to leave at this time and there would be no repercussions. There were no takers of this offer.

◊ ◊ ◊

During our in-processing we stayed at House 22, a safe house in downtown Da Nang where there was a bar and a grill where you could purchase sandwiches and hamburgers. There were even prostitutes available to service visiting guests.

A couple of days after the briefing, those of us assigned to FOB2 were flown to Kontum in II Corps, and we reported to the SOG compound just south of Kontum City on the road to Pleiku.

CHAPTER 5

FOB2/CCC Kontum

After I checked in at FOB2 in Kontum, I was assigned to the dispensary as a medic. I immediately asked to be re-assigned to a Spike Team but was advised I had to fill a medical slot because medics were critically needed. I was shown to the room I would share with S.Sgt. Gerald Denison, code name "Grommet," who had formerly run recon on ST Nevada and ST Ohio and was currently flying as a Covey Rider. "Covey" was the code name for Forward Air Control elements providing support for SOG missions. Covey Riders were typically ex-recon team leaders (One-Zeros) who flew with the Covey Pilots acting as spotters. Additionally, they coordinated communications with the teams on the ground and when necessary directed their movements. This left the pilot of the Covey plane free to concentrate on the flying.

Grommet was very kind to me and made me feel at home. He was especially helpful in acquainting me with the acronyms used in talking to the teams. He explained jargon such as "Spare 39er," (request for extraction); "37 Mike-Mike," (37-millimeter antiaircraft guns); and a whole range of other code words. This would assist me greatly in all of my future missions as a chase medic and while on recon.

◊ ◊ ◊

Denison had distinguished himself on ST Ohio when he was conducting a mission of area reconnaissance, road interdiction, and ambush in the Plei Trap Valley to the west of Kontum from 15 to 18 March, 1968. The

S.Sgt. Gerald Denison—code name "Grommet". (Robert Kotin photo)

team at that time consisted of One-Zero S.Sgt. Denison, One-One Sgt. Robert Kotin, and One-Two Sp5c. Francis Ruane.

On the evening of March 15, with heavy enemy movement as close as 20 meters, Denison held his position and called in artillery fire on the enemy locations resulting in vehicle destruction and secondary explosions. On March 17, the team located a well-traveled enemy supply route and proceeded to set up an ambush using Claymore mines and white phosphorous grenades. After moving a short distance from the target area, the lead vehicle of a 10-truck convoy hit the mines, destroying the lead vehicle and killing two enemy soldiers. Denison elected to sit tight and direct artillery fire on the convoy with artillery rounds landing as close as 50 meters from the team's position. Denison remained at the location to get a more complete damage assessment despite knowing that the enemy would soon be searching the area for forward observers.

For their efforts, Denison and Kotin received Bronze Star Medals for Valor and Ruane was awarded the Army Commendation Medal for Valor.

◊ ◊ ◊

Spike Team Ohio, early 1968. Americans at right end: Gerald Denison (L) and S.Sgt. Robert Kotin (R). (Robert Kotin photo)

I reported to the dispensary the day after my arrival at FOB2 and met S.Sgt. John Probart, the medical supervisor. He was a friendly individual whose medical knowledge I would eventually come to regard akin to that of a doctor. I asked him about transferring to a Spike Team, but he said I was needed in the dispensary. He also told me I would have opportunities to alternate those duties with flying chase medic and accompanying Hatchet Force and SLAM operations when they came up.

It disappointed me greatly that I was so close to being in a position to fight the enemy and would now be relegated to a support role. I resigned myself to the fact that this would be my job. I was going to be a *bac si*—a medic. In Vietnamese, *bac si* literally means "doctor," but everyone called the medics that name, most of the time, and it was meant to be complimentary.

Aerial photo of FOB2. (Paul Morris photo)

I was not the only new arrival at FOB2 who was not assigned to recon as he would have preferred. Bob Garcia, who went through the briefing at Da Nang with me, was sent to the commo bunker. There were a number of commo men who would much rather have been on recon. Since we all had a common gripe, we formed what amounted to an unofficial support group and would gather together in the club many nights bitching about our plight. Some of these included, in addition to Garcia, Larry Stephens, Billy Simmons, Ron Bozikis, William Copley, and Ken Worthley. I had spent much of the time on my flight to Vietnam playing hearts with Stephens and a couple of other SF personnel.

◊ ◊ ◊

During the evenings when I was in my room, Grommet would return from his Covey Rider duties, and quite often other Covey Riders would stop by to discuss the day's missions. Paul Poole, who like Denison had finished his stint on recon, was a close friend of Grommet and almost a

S.Sgt. Paul Poole at FOB2, 1968. (Robert Kotin photo)

Dallas Longstreath with ST Illinois in Target Lima 6, Laos, April 1968. (Dallas Longstreath photo)

nightly visitor. He had previously run recon with several teams including Colorado and Texas with Clarence "Pappy" Webb. He earned a Silver Star, Bronze Star for Valor, and Army Commendation for Valor on these recon missions in February and March 1968. Paul would later distinguish himself as a member of the Son Tay prison raid in North Vietnam in November 1970.

Dallas Longstreath was another Covey Rider who would come by our room on a regular basis. Dallas had previously put in his time on Spike Teams Florida and Illinois, serving as One-Zero of the latter until March/April 1968. Dallas was the only person at FOB2 I knew whose code name was the same as his real name. When I asked him how he got the code name "Dallas," he said that it was the one he chose to use and simply had ignored the one assigned to him.

I eagerly eavesdropped on their conversations. It was like hearing a nightly news commentary on the day's operations. After I started flying as a chase medic, I soon learned that orbiting at 8,000 feet aboard the chase ship often left me in the dark concerning many aspects of what was happening close to and on the ground. Many times, insertion and

FOB2 dispensary in background. (Paul Morris photo)

American personnel (L–R): Sgt. Ronald Brown, Sfc. John L. Probart (supervisor), Sgt. William Lensch, Sp4c. James D. Howes. (Bryon Loucks photo)

extraction ships were coming under fire and from my vantage point I was totally unaware that anything was happening. But the Covey Pilots and Riders were always right in the middle of the action.

◊ ◊ ◊

The dispensary was a relatively large building divided into seven rooms. There was a reception room where sick call was conducted, an operating room, a long ward wing with about 30 beds, a laboratory with a microscope for performing medical lab tests, a back room with shower, a storeroom, and a small living quarters that slept three of the medics. Duties in the dispensary included conducting sick call in the mornings for our American and indigenous personnel and their dependents, performing minor surgery, suturing, doing lab work such as blood exams to diagnose malaria cases, and various other related medical procedures.

Indigenous medical personnel assigned to FOB2/CCC in 1968. Back row (L–R): Yen, two unidentified Montagnard assistants, Thuong (Baby San), Hang (Pocahontas), and interpreter An. Front row (L–R): Thinh, Tan, Ut, and Bui Ngoc Tuan ("Chief"), medical supervisor. (Bryon Loucks photo)

Another person assigned to the dispensary was Sgt. Bill Lensch, also an extremely proficient medic. He loved to give me duties that showcased my inexperience and made me aware that I was the "green" medic. I never minded this since the result always forced me to learn something new and made me better at what I was there to do. Three more American medics worked in the dispensary, including one whose tour was getting short. He sold me his small refrigerator for $120 to use on his R&R.

There were a number of Vietnamese civilians paid by SOG who worked in the dispensary with the American medics. The interpreter was An, who had been a student at the University of Saigon prior to the war. He had the best command of the English language of any of the interpreters I met during my tour. He was a math whiz who knew calculus and would be a savior to me when I conducted sick call. The knowledge he gained while serving as interpreter made him probably more qualified than I was to work as a medic in the dispensary.

Bui Ngoc Tuan (nicknamed "Chief") was the Vietnamese medical supervisor, and he oversaw all of the Vietnamese medics, nurses, and assistants. His sister-in-law, a young Vietnamese named Hang Pham, also worked in the dispensary. He kept a close eye on her to be sure she did not fall into one of the Americans' clutches. She was a good girl, unlike many of the Vietnamese women, and we always called her *Co* Hang (Miss Hang) out of respect. Rumor had it that she attended Catholic services daily. This only made the Americans desire her even more. She wore her hair in long pigtails and was given the nickname "Pocahontas." To my knowledge, Tuan was successful in his efforts to protect his sister-in-law, and no American was able to partake of the forbidden fruit.

In addition, there were three Vietnamese medics and six Vietnamese nurses. The 4th Division firebase south of us on the road to Pleiku, Fire Support Base Mary Lou, had X-ray and dental capabilities that we could utilize for procedures beyond the scope of the dispensary. Slightly further south of Mary Lou, approximately three and a half miles from the FOB, was the 'Yard camp that housed some of our Montagnard companies. The 'Yard camp also had a couple of medics assigned to it and received its medical supplies from the FOB2 dispensary. The 'Yard camp was originally built to separate the Montagnards from the Vietnamese LLDB and Chinese Nungs at FOB2 since they did not generally get along well. The Montagnards were, for the most part, looked down upon by the Oriental Vietnamese.

◊ ◊ ◊

But flying chase medic would be the part of my job I enjoyed the most. It allowed me to be involved in the action and provided a bird's-eye view of the Spike Teams' insertions and extractions into and from the field. Recon insertions and extractions were generally conducted with eight helicopters—four gunships and four slicks (passenger-carrying ships) being deployed. The Covey Pilot and Covey Rider coordinated the operations and generally kept tactical air support on station during the missions.

The helicopters were either Hueys, flown by U.S. pilots, or "Kingbees," flown by Vietnamese pilots and crews. The tactical air elements varied from jets to Spads (single-engine A1-Es and A1-Hs). They could provide support with rockets, both high explosive and fleshette; cluster bombs; hard bombs; white phosphorous bombs; machine guns and cannons; as well as napalm.

The U.S. Army Assault Helicopter Companies supporting FOB2/CCC during my tour were the 57th AHC with their "Gladiator" slicks and "Cougar" Cobra and Huey gunships; the 119th AHC with their "Gator" slicks and "Croc" Huey gunships; the 170th AHC with their "Bikini" slicks and "Buccaneer" Huey gunships; the 189th AHC with their "Ghostrider" slicks and "Avenger" Huey gunships; and the Air Force 20th Special Operations Squadron with their "Green Hornet" Hueys. Cobra gunship support also came from the 361st Aviation Company (Escort) aka "The Pink Panthers."

One of the four slicks was designated the "chase" ship for each mission. It was on this helicopter that the chase medic rode, along with the pilot, co-pilot, crew chief, and door gunner. The chase ship generally orbited at 8,000 feet above the activity and occasionally would go down to pick up part of a team. This happened most frequently when someone on the ground was wounded and required immediate first aid while being flown to the nearest American medical facility.

Usually two of the four slicks were rigged with 120-foot ropes for rappel-in insertions or McGuire rig extractions. Later in my tour, 60-foot "rope ladders" made from steel cable with aluminum rungs were introduced. I often wondered, but never asked, how the chase ship was selected as there never seemed to be any particular reason. Some days the chase ship would be one of those rigged with ropes, other days it would be one without ropes. Although the chase ship did not normally participate in the team pickups unless someone was wounded, there were numerous exceptions.

The chase medic had the option of going to the mission briefings beforehand, where he would be advised of the "pushes" for the day (FM radio frequency and alternate) or he could get them from the pilots when they boarded the helicopters. At first, I attended the briefings, but then realized that if our helicopter was shot down, I would have far more knowledge of the teams on the ground than I needed. I feared that if I was captured, I might crack under torture and provide information that could compromise teams on missions. I stopped going to the briefings after a month or so, figuring the less I knew about the details of ongoing missions, the better.

Bill Lensch assisted me in preparing my gear for flying as a chase medic. The web gear was the same as that carried by the Spike Teams. We carried M-16s and a load of approximately 400 rounds of ammunition. We also carried six fragmentation grenades, two smoke grenades, a marking panel, pen flare, strobe light, signal mirror, compass, sling rope for making a Swiss seat, URC-10 survival radio, and combat knife; plus four canteens of water—two on the web gear and two in the side pockets of our rucksacks.

As chase medic, aside from my web gear and M-16, I brought mostly medical supplies with me to provide immediate first aid. These were carried in the same kind of rucksack as that used by the Spike Teams. A few of the items included a 1,000cc bottle of Ringer's lactate blood substitute, three cans of plasma (serum albumin), 40 to 50 combat dressings of various sizes, triangular bandages, adrenaline and heart needles, cannula and scalpel for doing a cricothyroidotomy, and miscellaneous items such as hemostats, bandage scissors, tape, etc.

We carried chloroquine to treat fever from malaria and morphine to relieve severe pain, along with medications to treat minor pain, fever, diarrhea, constipation, and a variety of other ailments. The job of the chase medic was relatively simple—to keep the wounded alive until they could be taken to more capable medical facilities. This became the basis for all future self-critiques of my own performance. If I got the patient to the medical facility alive, I had done my job.

Another critical piece of equipment the chase medic carried was a PRC-25 radio. This radio could be utilized in the initial launch of operations and served as a replacement for teams on the ground if theirs went out. When I first started flying chase medic duty in May 1968 we would fly from FOB2 in Kontum and land at the launch site at Dak To to await launch orders from the Covey Rider. The backup PRC-25

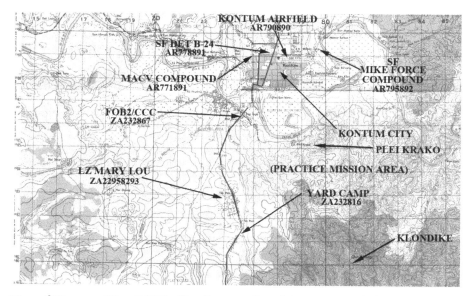

Map of Kontum City, FOB2, Fire Support Base Mary Lou, and the 'Yard Camp. (Map by Joe Parnar)

served as the means of communications because the helicopters would shut down, and when they shut down, so did their radios.

At that time, there was no permanent launch site at Dak To so everyone would return to the FOB at the end of the day. A typical scenario would be to fly to Dak To, move to the side of the runway, then run a commo check with Leghorn or the Covey Rider to be sure the radio was functioning properly. Leghorn was a permanently manned radio relay site located on a mountaintop about eight miles inside Laos.

The dialogue would go something like this:

"Grommet, Grommet, this is Strip, Strip—Over." (Strip was the call sign the chase medics used at Dak To.)

Grommet would reply, "Strip, this is Grommet—Go"

"Grommet this is Strip, commo check—Over."

Grommet would answer, "Strip, this is Grommet, I hear you five by, how me?—Over."

I would answer, "Grommet, this is Strip, I hear you Lima Charlie (loud and clear)—Over."

Grommet might then respond with, "Strip this is Grommet, what are your assets? —Over."

The reply might be, "Grommet, this is Strip, I have four turtles (code name for slicks), two snakes (Cobra gunships), and two hares (Huey gunships)—Over."

Grommet would end the conversation by saying, "Strip, this is Grommet, stand by for launch—Out."

I would monitor the radio for as long as it took to get the launch order. When word came to "launch your assets," I would whistle to get the pilots' attention and stand up and wave my arm around my head simulating a helicopter rotor. The pilots would immediately board their aircraft and start their engines. After the ships were running and they had established commo with Covey, my role was done.

I attempted to monitor conversations between the Covey Rider and the team during an insertion or extraction, but to hear anything over the noise of the engines and rotors, I had to block my right ear with the palm of my hand and press the handset tightly against my left ear. If the commo was not clear, it was difficult to make out any of the conversations. If we went down to pick up part of a team, I would put aside the handset and hold my M-16 at the ready to return enemy fire. With the PRC-25, I could only monitor the pilot's or Covey Rider's FM conversations with the team on the ground as the air asset pilots used other radio bands to communicate with one another.

Chase medics had a ringside seat for the missions. I often wondered why the FOB commanding officer did not come along so he could get a better feel for a team's situation and the terrain they were operating in. This would have given him better information to take into account when issuing orders and instructions to them. I later learned that the powers above him prohibited him from doing this.

Some of the FOB commanders, like Lieutenant Colonel Abt in the latter part of my tour, would occasionally fly over operations in the FAC planes to direct missions. I am sure MACV-SOG headquarters in Saigon would not have been pleased had they been informed.

Bill Lensch accompanied me the first time I flew chase in order to show me what to do. The insertions and extractions that day went without incident, so his instructions were minimal. During my first month flying chase, nothing of any significance happened. We picked up a number of teams, but there was never any enemy fire. On the days I worked in the dispensary, the chase medic that day after returning would quite frequently relate that they had picked up a team under fire and their ship was all shot up. After a couple of weeks, I began to doubt what I was hearing and figured that maybe they were mistaking for gun-shots the cracking sounds the rotors sometimes made as they slapped the air. I didn't realize I was simply riding a streak of beginner's luck.

The streak did not last long.

CHAPTER 6

The Loss of John Kedenburg

I was flying chase medic on June 13, 1968, when John Kedenburg was killed. The target area was Juliett 3, to the south and east of the "Bra" in southern Laos. The Bra was composed of several such hot target areas and had received its name from the way the double curvature of the Xe Xou River (*Dak Xou* in Vietnamese) in one place was said by the Americans to resemble a woman's bustline. Highway 110, a major artery of the Ho Chi Minh Trail, crossed Juliett 3 from northwest to southeast. North of the road a high mountain range rose, and to the south there were relatively steep rolling hills. The terrain on both sides of the road was double and triple canopy jungle. The area was a couple of kilometers north of the abandoned village of Ban Pakha where Highways 96/110 split apart.

Team Nevada, led by One-Zero Sp5c. John Kedenburg, had been inserted on June 12 to conduct surveillance of Highway 96/110 and call in airstrikes on any truck traffic they might observe. The One-One on the mission was Sp5c. Stephen Roche who had joined Nevada a month earlier. In addition, there were eight indigenous personnel with Kedenburg and Roche. The following day, as they neared Highway 96/110, the team made contact with a large force of NVA.

They backtracked the way they had come and headed for some bomb craters they had passed earlier. Kedenburg lagged behind to provide rearguard action to slow down the enemy pursuit as Roche and the rest of the team proceeded towards the craters. While fleeing from the enemy, one of the team's indigenous personnel became separated from the rest

The Bra was a hot target area abutting Juliett 9 and Hotel 9 in Laos. (Luke Dove photo)

of the team and was presumed dead. Kedenburg caught up with the team at the bomb craters and requested an extraction. The NVA arrived shortly thereafter and a firefight ensued during which one indigenous team member was KIA.

The Covey Rider that day was Gerald Denison, "Grommet." Providing helicopter support, was the 189th Assault Helicopter Company, the Ghostriders, and their gunships, the Avengers.

The first rescue helicopter attempted to land under intense enemy fire, but was forced to abandon the effort due to the dense foliage surrounding the LZ. Grommet called in airstrikes by A1-E Skyraiders and utilized the Avenger gunships in an attempt to suppress the enemy fire to no avail. He then decided to extract the team by McGuire rig—120-foot ropes with leg loops dropped from the chopper into which the team would put their legs and hold onto the rope or snap-link it to their upper web harness.

The chase ship I rode on was one of the two Huey slicks on the mission that were equipped with ropes for McGuire rig (string) extraction.

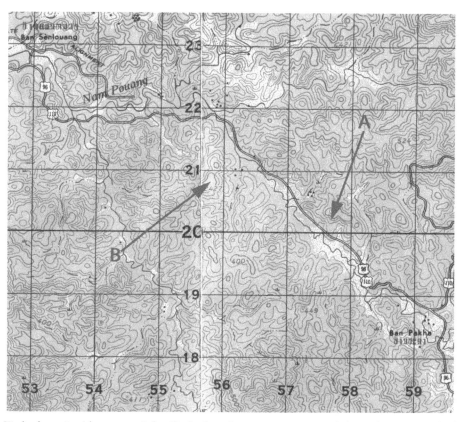

Kedenburg incident map. John Kedenburg's team was extracted from the area marked "A" which is in southern Laos. The "B" marks the location of the .51-caliber machine gun that was firing at the extraction Hueys. (Map by Joe Parnar)

A second rescue ship hovering above a small opening in the 80-foot bamboo tree tops took heavy enemy fire, but was able to successfully extract four of the team's indigenous members by means of the McGuire rigs.

The third extraction ship, the one I was on, was next up. As we came to a hover over the LZ, the crew chief and the door gunner lay down prone on the floor of the chopper to lower the ropes to the team and direct the pilots. The crew chief had previously informed me the team was on the run with the NVA hot on their tail and one of their team members was missing.

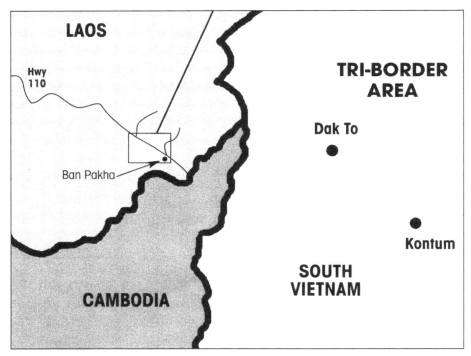

Map showing relationship of Kedenburg incident to tri-border junction. (From original edition of *SOG Medic* by Paladin Press)

I was seated on the floor of the chopper facing out the left side when we started taking .51-caliber machine gun fire directly from our rear at approximately 2,000 meters distance. The gun was located on the hillside across the road to our northwest. I could see streaks from the tracers and hear the crackling of the rounds as they passed under the rotor blades about eight feet outside the left door. Fortunately, we were giving the shooter the poorest profile of the ship at which to aim. Had we been broadside, we probably would have been shot down.

There was a ridgeline at eye level east of where I was sitting roughly 30 meters from our hovering Huey. I sat with my rifle pointed in that direction when a person suddenly appeared, flapping a red panel at our chopper. I shook the crew chief's ankle to get his attention and pointed to the ridgeline, but when I looked up the person and panel were gone. He motioned for me to use my weapon, but I assumed the

John Kedenburg surrounded by his ST Nevada teammates, May 1968. (Photo taken by George Wilson Hunt and supplied by Mary Jane Kedenburg)

panel flapper was the missing team member. He made no attempt to shoot at our Huey and I did not have time to explain the details of the situation to the crew chief. With the roar of the engines and crackling of the rounds passing close to our ship, he wouldn't have heard what I was saying anyway, even if I was shouting into his ear.

We hovered for what seemed like an eternity and the pilot maintained his position. Finally, as the fire intensified, the pilot had to abruptly pull out, inadvertently dragging those on the ropes below through the trees.

Once clear of the trees, we beelined it for the airstrip at the isolated Special Forces camp at Ben Het, where those on the strings would be eased to the ground. After the chopper landed, I had a chance to evaluate the injuries. The first thing I discovered was that there were only three individuals in the strings and John Kedenburg was not among them. The other American on Nevada, Sp5c. Roche, had cuts and scratches on his face from the tree branches. His face was smeared with dried blood, but he said he was OK. Roche reported that Kedenburg had given up his seat to a late-arriving team member. When the chopper suddenly pulled out, Kedenburg was left behind and had remained on the ground alone.

Of the two indigenous team members who made it out successfully, the first appeared to also have only cuts and scratches, but the second one had been whacked in the head by a tree limb and had unequal pupils, a sign of intracranial pressure on the brain. We carried the unconscious man to the chopper and loaded him on board, then flew to the 4th Division medical facility at Dak To. The fate of the other indigenous team member, who should have been in the fourth string, was not known. He may have been ripped off his rope when dragged through the trees, especially if he was not fully secured.

When we arrived at Dak To, the 4th Division medics transferred the injured indigenous team member onto a stretcher and carried him to their underground medical bunker. I started to follow them when Roche asked me if he could go along to see if his teammate would be all right.

I said, "OK, come on," but would later regret the decision.

When we entered the medical bunker, a medic at a desk at the foot of the ramp began to ask me a series of questions. Roche helped me with the name of the indigenous team member and then, seeing the blood on Roche's face, one of the leg medics realized they had a wounded American. I told them I had evaluated Roche and he was OK and we would clean him up back at our base.

At that point, the medic asking the questions wanted to know where the incident had happened. I wasn't expecting the question, so I replied that we were on a top secret mission and I could not divulge the location. A 4th Division captain, overhearing my response, approached and said, "What do you mean you can't tell us where it happened?" He demanded my name, rank, and serial number, which I gave to him. By this time, they were ready to lead Roche to a cot to clean him up.

Since I had not sterilized Roche (taken away his codebook, map, and notes), I wasn't about to let him go, because sterilizing a person we dropped off was part of the chase medic's responsibilities. I shouted over to Roche, "Let's get out of here!" and we started up the ramp.

Sp5c. Stephen M. Roche of ST Nevada, who served on recon teams and Hatchet Force. (Bryon Loucks photo)

The captain followed us, yelling, "You'll hear from us, 'top secret'! You can't come in here and take a patient out! You'll hear from us, 'top secret'!"

I was so shaken that when we got back on the helicopter I started trying to explain to one of the crewmembers what had happened so that he could back up my story. All at once a black major from the 4th Division ran up to our ship, pointed a finger in my face, and screamed, "Don't you ever come into our medical bunker again." He then stomped away. We lifted off and returned to our holding area off to the south side of the main airstrip. We got no further word on Kedenburg and later a chopper flew us back to Kontum.

I was still shaken by the incident and told Sgt. Maj. Rupert G. Stratton about it when we arrived. He advised me to go and report it to Lt. Col. Donald L. ("Whiskey") Smith, the FOB2 commanding officer at that time.

Colonel Smith listened to the story and told me I had done the right thing. His comment was "Fuck those legs! If anything comes down on this, it is going right in there," and pointed into his wastebasket. He then dismissed me.

◊ ◊ ◊

The next day a Bright Light (rescue) team consisting of Sfc. Sherman Batman, Sp5c. Mike Tramel, Sgt. Bryon Loucks (a classmate of mine from SF Medic training), Sp5c. Thomas Cunningham, and several indigenous personnel from ST Illinois were inserted to try to find John Kedenburg. Grommet was again flying Covey. It was my day to work in the dispensary and we later received word that the team had recovered Kedenburg's body and was in heavy contact. They were successfully extracted just before dark and arrived at the dispensary later that evening. One of the indigenous team members was KIA/BNR (body not recovered) and most of the team was wounded, including Batman, Loucks, Tramel, and Cunningham.

Kedenburg was taken into the back room of the dispensary, where the shower was located. Sgt. Bill Lensch said that since I was the newest medic, it would be my job to clean up his body and prepare it for shipment back to the States. Lensch led me into the room where Kedenburg was and told me to remove his clothes and wash him, and he would return later to show me how to finish the procedures.

I was never an overly religious person, but I remembered the story of someone telling Christ that they were not worthy to loosen the thongs of his sandals. This is how I felt as I unlaced John's boots. There in the room with his body, a passage I had heard somewhere from the Bible echoed in my brain. "No greater love has one man for another, than he will give up his life for his friend." I was glad Lensch had left me alone as I removed John's jungle fatigues, and it hit me how devastated my family would be if this were me. I realized it was going to be equally devastating for John's family. Silent tears rolled down my cheeks and once again I was thankful I was alone. Grave doubts crept into my mind that maybe I had volunteered myself right out of my league. I wondered, if I had been in the same position, would I have given up my life for one of my teammates? Also, I now wanted more than ever to get on a Spike Team and kill some NVA.

John Kedenburg would later be posthumously awarded the Medal of Honor for his heroic, unselfish actions the previous day. Washing his body and preparing him for shipment back to the States is the greatest honor I have ever had.

◊ ◊ ◊

Later on, in the club, I got my first introduction to a SOG tradition to honor troops missing or killed in action. Throughout the evening, the conversations were mostly about Kedenburg, until toward the end of the evening, when someone began singing the folk song "Hey, Blue," slowly and sadly. Everyone joined in. The last line of the song substituted Kedenburg's name for "Blue" and ended with "Hey, Kedenburg, you were a good guy, you." I didn't dare look into anyone else's eyes, but I suspect they were as teary as my own. On this occasion, having left John's body a short time before, there was a finality and verification of his death. On subsequent singings of "Hey, Blue" to missing or killed men, I often had the faint hope that maybe they were still alive or word of their death was only a rumor. But when you saw the bodies of the men, you knew their deaths were a fact.

◊ ◊ ◊

It wasn't long after that I was flying chase and we picked up some Montagnards who had been burned in a napalm strike a team had called in to break enemy contact. Their wounds were serious enough that we had to go to the nearest medical facility, which in this case was my dreaded 4th Division medical bunker at Dak To, from which I had been banned.

The procedure was the same as my first visit. A medic at the desk began asking me questions and filling out a form to process the wounded Montagnards. I explained I did not know their names. As I was being asked the location of the incident, I hesitated and then saw the same captain approaching whom I had had the run-in with before.

I said to myself, "Oh, shit. Here we go again."

But this time the captain told the clerk, "Leave that question blank," and in a most pleasant manner he asked me if I would be at Dak To the following day. He even volunteered to keep the wounded Montagnards there overnight to be sure they were stable. I could pick them up and take them back to our base the next day. I accepted the offer and never had another problem at that facility.

CHAPTER 7

ST Texas, June–July 1968

I was on duty in the dispensary conducting sick call, when Major Smith, the recon company commander and who I knew had considerable clout, entered. I got him aside and asked and even pleaded with him to get me on a recon team. He said he would look into it and get back to me. Two days later he returned and advised me there was nothing he could do. I was exceedingly disappointed and again became unhappy that I would be relegated to the dispensary and flying chase medic for the balance of my tour.

My disappointment was so great that I did the only thing I could think of to get relief. I went to the club after working hours and got drunk and cried in my beer. It was during one of my feeling-sorry-for-myself binges that I met Sfc. Clarence H. "Pappy" Webb, One-Zero of Spike Team Texas. Pappy listened to my sob story while I paid for the beers for both of us throughout the evening. Actually, I don't think Pappy really cared all that much about me or my problems. He had a Vietnamese woman he lived with who had two small children and he kept a rented apartment for them just outside the wire of the FOB2 compound. The financial drain of this, as well as the fact that he had a wife in the States who received a good chunk of his pay, made him favorably disposed toward anyone who would buy him drinks.

I did know one thing: everyone at FOB2 respected Pappy from the commander on down. During his multiple tours with SOG, his bravery and willingness to go into the hottest targets was unquestioned.

From left: David Gilmer, Joe Parnar, and Clarence "Pappy" Webb at the Dak To launch facility. (Bryon Loucks photo)

Toward the end of the evening Pappy looked me directly in the eyes and asked, "Parnar, do you really want to get on a recon team?"

I told him I wanted that more than anything and he said he would see what he could do. I really didn't have a great deal of hope. I figured if Major Smith with his clout could not make it happen, what could Pappy do?

I was working the next day at the dispensary when Major Smith came in and told me to move my gear into the ST Texas team room, Pappy's team. He explained that Pappy had a medic on his team who had three months left in-country and wanted off recon. I was swapping places with him. I almost gave the major a big kiss. I thanked him profusely while realizing how much pull Pappy had as a recon team leader.

When I began moving my things into the team room, I met Pappy's One-One, Sp4c. Paul L. Morris, Jr. Paul was from Stoughton, Massachusetts, about 70 miles from my home town, and we hit it off well together. He had dropped out of college as I had done, having attended

Paul Morris (on right) was the One-One of ST Texas. (Paul Morris photo)

Holy Cross College. Paul had been a football player in college and was a large man. I wondered to myself how I would ever carry him if he got wounded on a mission.

Morris filled me in on Team Texas and informed me I was not to take any photographs of Pappy, as he was sensitive about having his picture taken. I figured that with the nature of our work, he probably didn't want any pictures of himself floating around that the enemy could use in order to produce wanted posters of him. Morris told me how Pappy and his Vietnamese woman, Leiah, had come together. He said Pappy was running an operation when one of his indigenous personnel was wounded. When he opened up his shirt to treat him, Pappy discovered an ace bandage flattening out what proved to be breasts—his team member was a woman disguised as a man. Her husband was an ARVN pilot who had been killed, and she was posing as a man to try to kill

The indigenous personnel of ST Texas, shown in 1968. (Paul Morris photo)

NVA and Vietcong to avenge his death. In addition, she found the pay working for Americans enabled her to better provide for her two small children. I guess this kind of grit had won the admiration of Pappy as he and Leiah ended up living together outside the FOB2 compound with her two children.

Paul Morris also related that Pappy had told him of an indigenous team member named Tiet, who had once come to Pappy in tears saying he would have to quit the team. He said that the local VC had come to his house and threatened to do harm to his wife and eight children if he did not kill Pappy. According to Paul, Pappy and Tiet went to Tiet's house, and a couple of nights later they eliminated the threat when the VC returned.

◊ ◊ ◊

The next few days were spent getting my gear set up and training with my team. We rehearsed immediate action drills and breaking an ambush. We

Bryon Loucks, One-Zero of ST Washington, holds Pappy Webb's banana cat (civet). (Bryon Loucks photo)

practiced with live fire at the rifle range near the Montagnard compound a few miles south of the FOB.

Texas drew a mission, but Pappy decided to take only a small team into the field. I stayed behind because I was the green man. Paul and Pappy conducted the mission without making contact. Afterward, Paul told me that Pappy was very unpredictable in the woods, sometimes walking down the trails and at other times heading up the steepest hills or into the thickest jungle. That may have been the secret of his success at running recon. The enemy could not anticipate his movements.

While Pappy and Paul were on the mission, I was alone in the team room. I had my newly acquired CAR-15—a submachine gun version of the M-16 with a collapsible stock—the indispensable weapon for any recon man. I decided to make a sling for mine by braiding three lengths of parachute suspension line together. When it was done, I put my weapon over my shoulders to see how it fit. Feeling somewhat like John Wayne, I was fantasizing about being in contact with the enemy and accidentally pulled the trigger. Unfortunately, the safety was off, and I shot a three-inch-deep hole in the concrete lower portion of the wall to the left of the door. All I remember was the sound of the discharge and then being showered by chips of concrete. A cloud of dust rose and spread to every corner of the room. A minute later, Bryon Loucks came running in wondering if anyone had been shot. I sheepishly explained that I had accidentally fired off a round while trying out my new sling. He told me to be careful, as firing a round without cause on the compound could lead to a $50 fine. I spent the next hour sweeping the floor and cleaning the room to remove all of the concrete chips and dust. I never told Pappy or Paul about the incident, but years later, Paul would remark that he recalled seeing the hole but never knew where it came from.

◊ ◊ ◊

During one of our stand-down days, we went to the PX. Pappy checked out a Deuce-and-a-half from the motor pool and strapped a jug of Montagnard rice wine, complete with bamboo straws, on the right front fender where the extra fuel can would normally go. While Paul and I rode in the open back of the truck, Leiah sat in the cab with Pappy. He picked up a couple of legs from the 4th Division who were hitchhiking. A little later Pappy was just driving along when he suddenly stopped. He shut off the truck, got out of the cab, slowly walked around to the jug of rice wine, and took a sip. He then slowly walked back to the cab, got in, started the truck, and continued driving on. One of the legs asked us if he had stopped the truck just to take a sip. Paul and I responded, "Of course, he's thirsty."

On another one of our other trips to the PX, we stopped at a Buddhist temple in downtown Kontum on the way back. At some point in his life, Pappy had adopted Buddhism as his religion. We went inside and Pappy showed us around and introduced us to the monk who ran the temple. When we got back to the Jeep we were using, someone had stolen the items Paul Morris had purchased at the PX. I had never seen Pappy look so pissed, but the thieves had already long since departed.

Lesson learned: Never leave things unattended in the Jeep when you go downtown.

The apartment that Pappy rented for himself and his Vietnamese family was just outside the wire of the FOB on the north edge of the compound. Paul and I visited him there on a couple of occasions. Pappy had a pet "banana cat" (civet) that he let run loose inside the apartment. It would tightrope walk along the cord from which some blankets hung to divide the large single room into two sections. I became afraid of the creature after it once bit Pappy on the finger when he was teasing it. I never was able to get used to that and only went to see him in his apartment when I had to.

Probably the scariest thing that happened while I was on ST Texas was when Pappy and Paul Morris returned from a recon mission and Pappy got word that some of the officers had been messing around with Leiah and making passes at her. Pappy came back from the club drunk one night and gave orders to myself and to Paul.

He said, "Parnar, I want you to go to the corner bunker and get a can of M-60 machine gun ammo. Morris, I want you to hang a belt to hold my M-60 machine gun from the ceiling. I'm going to go to my hooch outside the wire and get my M-60 and I'm going to level this compound."

I got the ammo and Paul hung the belt, and we stayed up all night praying Pappy would not return. It was a real touchy situation. On the one hand, Pappy, being One-Zero of the team, was God and we had to follow his orders. On the other hand, obeying them would have gotten us all court-martialed had he returned and carried out his threat. Luckily, he never came back and mention of the incident was never made again.

◊ ◊ ◊

One day shortly after I joined the team, Pappy announced that he and I were going to Pleiku to obtain our monthly food rations from the distribution center. He drove a three-quarter-ton truck that was painted black and had a large wooden box built onto the back. The FOB had also sent a second truck with duplicate food requisitions to try to double up on the food allocation. Pappy brought Leiah along on the trip. Because of the narrow, steeply crowned roads we had to travel on, and because our whole rig appeared to be top-heavy, there were times when I thought for sure we would tip over. But we made it. Leiah visited some friends she had in Pleiku while Pappy and I went to get the food.

I got my first real taste of Special Forces scrounging while on this excursion. At the distribution center, we drove between row upon row of canned goods and foodstuffs sitting on pallets in an open-air, pavilion-like structure that had a roof overhead but no surrounding walls. In one instance, Pappy told the leg on duty we needed two cases of #10 cans of string beans. The leg said that they were two rows over and went to retrieve them. Pappy told him he would be there in a minute to help him since it was only the two cases. After waiting for the leg to get out of hearing distance, Pappy said we could use a few cases of some other items that were stacked nearby. While the two of them were getting the string beans, I threw as many cases of the other items as I could into the truck before they returned. We must have left with twice as many canned goods as we were allocated. All of this was in addition to the other truck with the duplicate requisition. When we stopped to get our meat allocation the clerk checked the paperwork carefully and declared that the other truck had already picked it up. So, no double meat ration.

We met Leiah and drove back to Kontum. I held my breath the entire way, hoping we wouldn't tip over whenever we swerved to the right to miss a truck coming from the opposite direction. We made it back without incident, although Pappy pointed out numerous places where convoys had been ambushed.

Upon arriving at the FOB, we parked behind the mess hall. While Pappy was talking to the NCO in charge about getting someone to help unload the truck, I went to the cab where Pappy and I had stored our CAR-15s. I grabbed mine and headed back to the team room. Little did I know how badly I had screwed up.

The next morning Pappy came to the team room. "Where is my CAR-15?" he demanded.

I replied that the last time I saw it was when I had taken mine out of the cab of the truck in the rear loading area of the mess hall. Pappy was so mad he was nearly trembling. He shook his clenched fist in my face and said, "If you ever do that again—"

He did not need to explain why. It dawned on me hard and fast that as a member of a recon team, you are responsible for everything. Had I not said I last saw his weapon on the truck, he might have been easier on me. I realized that it was everyone's duty on a recon team to look after all the weapons, even if they were not one's own.

My only response was, "I'm sorry, Pappy, it will never happen again!"

"It had better not," was all he said.

Another lesson learned the hard way.

◊ ◊ ◊

On July 3, when we were getting ready to leave for the 'Yard camp for training, Pappy told Paul Morris and me, "It was one year ago today we lost Seymour (Sfc. Leo E. Seymour) in Charlie 7, in Laos." He said they had been pinning some propaganda posters to trees when the team was

The entrance to the 'Yard camp. The tower can be seen in the center of the photo. (Paul Morris photo)

hit and got split up. Seymour was never heard from again. It seemed a little creepy knowing someone from our team had become MIA exactly one year ago to the day.

◊ ◊ ◊

I had been with the team about three weeks when Pappy announced that we were to be trained in static-line parachuting from helicopters to give us an additional insertion capability. We conducted the training at the 'Yard camp where there were some crude platforms we jumped from while learning parachute landing falls. The job of demonstrating the proper method of rolling after landing from front, rear, and side falls went to me. The training consisted mostly of parachute landing falls since there were no towers we could use to practice exiting from the choppers.

A few days later I was informed by Pappy that I was being transferred to Spike Team Ohio. I was very disappointed because I would not be making a night practice jump with Team Texas. At first, I thought that it might have been a result of my screw-up involving Pappy's CAR-15,

The 'Yard camp as seen from the tower inside the camp. (Paul Morris photo)

The training area at the 'Yard camp. (Paul Morris photo)

ST Texas's 2nd (daytime) training jump. (Bryon Loucks photo)

ST Texas team member landing in cornfield. (Bryon Loucks photo)

Paul Morris and teammate in cornfield after 2nd (daytime) training jump. (Bryon Loucks photo.)

but when I reported to the One-Zero of Ohio, I learned he was the only American left on the team. Also, since Pappy continued to be friendly to me, I assumed I was not transferred because I had gotten him mad.

Captain Edward Lesesne approached me as I was rounding up my gear to move to the Ohio team room and asked if I would provide medical coverage on the drop zone for the Team Texas night jump. I accepted without hesitation. In this way, I could be with them even if it was on the ground. Led by Captain Lesesne, we were trucked to the drop zone, which was roughly a 20-minute drive from FOB2. The jump was a success and no one was injured during the exercise. I really envied Pappy and Paul Morris for having had the opportunity to jump in Vietnam, even if it was a practice exercise.

The next day Texas made a day jump into a corn field near the local Catholic Church. Bryon Loucks took several photos of the jump. ST Texas was now jump qualified.

CHAPTER 8

ST Ohio, July 1968—First Mission

I moved my gear into the ST Ohio team room the next morning and met the One-Zero, S.Sgt. Robert C. Kotin. A very reserved individual, he was rather short and sported a handlebar mustache. Kotin informed me we were going on a walkout practice mission the following morning. He went over which pockets he wanted gear such as maps and the codebook carried in, but said little in the way of other things he expected on recon.

S.Sgt. Robert C. Kotin, ST Ohio One-Zero, July 1968. (Robert Kotin photo)

The next morning dawned bright and sunny and I was introduced to the indigenous team members. ST Ohio was a mixed team, with both Vietnamese and Montagnards as members. This was unusual since Montagnards and Vietnamese generally didn't get along well together. The three Montagnards were Het, the indigenous team sergeant; Hlock the tail gunner; and Mock, the M-79 grenadier. Het and Hlock were of the Jarai tribe and Mock was Rhade. The indigenous interpreter was a Mr. Tho (Nguyen Phung Tho) pronounced "Thah". We Americans called him "Toe" and that's how we always mispronounced his name. Tho had a fairly good command of the English language. Many of the Vietnamese on the team were young and liked to kid around. They immediately asked me if I would get them a case of Cokes at the PX when we returned from the mission. I said yes, not realizing that this would become standard practice on all future missions.

Since this would be my first time in the field, I decided to watch the indigenous team members and learn from them. I had trained with

ST Ohio Jarai Montagnard Het, 1968.
(Luke Dove photo)

ST Ohio Jarai Montagnard Hlock, 1968. (Robert Kotin photo)

ST Ohio Rhade Montagnard Mock, 1968. (Joe Parnar photo)

Team Texas, but that mostly involved immediate action drills for breaking contact and attacking an ambush. I had absolutely no idea how team members actually conducted themselves on operations, and this fact made me a little uneasy.

We left the FOB through the north gate and turned right. We headed east along a small road that skirted the northeast defensive perimeter of the compound. A short distance beyond was a Montagnard village that consisted of several houses built on stilts to raise the floors off the damp ground and keep the chickens and pigs and other livestock out of the dwellings.

After passing the village, we veered off the road into the jungle. The first thing that became apparent was that we were moving much more slowly than we had on any of my training missions back in the States. I watched Mock, one of the Montagnards, to see exactly where he put his feet and tried to follow his example, unless where he stepped caused some noise. I figured this was probably a good practice even though NVA mines would not be a problem on missions over the wire in Laos and Cambodia. The NVA, for the most part, did not mine their own backyards, although there was always the possibility of stepping on a toe popper mine set by one of our recon teams on a previous operation.

But, because this practice exercise was in Kontum, there was always the possibility of encountering Vietcong mines in the area.

I carried my "monkey see, monkey do" learning regimen one step further and observed how Mock negotiated obstacles such as going under or over logs and through brush. Mock moved very quietly and it was obvious that he had grown up in the jungle and knew it well.

On one occasion, as Mock moved under some low-hanging vines and brush, he pointed above his head toward a large, multicolored caterpillar about eight inches long and covered with one-inch spines. It was the largest caterpillar I had ever seen. As he pointed to it, he shook his head from side to side and made a hand signal that looked like an umpire making a safe call. I immediately knew he meant, "Don't touch this." I nodded that I understood and made sure that I stayed clear of the caterpillar.

After moving for another 45 minutes we took our first break. Up to now there had been no verbal communications by any of the team members. Instructions were entirely by hand signals. The command for stop was holding up a hand such as a traffic cop would do. The signal for break was a movement that mimed breaking an imaginary stick in one's hand. These signals were passed back down the line by each individual. If the One-Zero wanted the team to eat on a particular break, the signal was a motion that aped spooning food into one's mouth. If smoking was permitted, the signal was to pretend to puff on a cigarette with an affirmative nod. I was amazed at how easy it was to understand these signals despite the fact I was seeing them for the first time and had no instruction whatsoever on what they meant.

As we took our first break, I could see One-Zero Kotin sitting back against his rucksack writing in a notebook. I thought to myself how much like the movies this all was, to see a soldier taking a break, writing a letter home to his girlfriend, mother, or wife. (I would later face the consequences of my mistaken assumption when we returned from the field.)

I also developed an immediate appreciation for the fact that I was carrying 80 pounds of equipment and ammunition. It felt good to sit down, and getting up after the break required some adjustment in order to avoid falling over backward. I thought of combat movies where the soldiers leaped over logs while running into a hail of bullets while carrying only a canteen and a couple of ammo pouches. I realized that running in our situation would be more akin to a waddling jog. I wondered how anyone could carry a wounded teammate with all the gear we were lugging.

Around midday we took another break. Kotin approached me and took my codebook and encrypted a message. He handed me the coded message to radio back to the FOB. It was standard operating procedure (SOP) to send three messages per day—one in the early morning when the team was about to move out of their RON (remain overnight) position, one at midday, and one at the end of the day when the teams prepared to RON. Of course, if the team made contact with the enemy, messages were verbally sent to the Covey Pilot and Covey Rider to assist with air strikes and to coordinate team movement and extraction. In our case, our communications were radioed directly to the FOB, whose call sign at that time was "Diamond Head."

The codebooks we used were ingenious. The three-letter designations changed each day, so even if the enemy deciphered one day's message, the code would be completely different the next. A three-letter group, "XYZ" for example, could mean "will move to" on one day and might represent the word "north" or the number "1" the next. There were only two codebooks in existence for each mission. One was carried by the radio operator and one was back at the FOB. The books were arranged alphabetically into two sections: one section contained a listing of words, phrases, and numbers for encoding messages; and the other was arranged by the three-letter groupings to be used for decoding messages. With the infrequency of transmissions, I didn't see how the enemy could ever crack the codes.

We moved all day and prepared to RON shortly before dark. Kotin moved the team into a bamboo thicket where we cleared out a space large enough to lie down in. Kotin then coded up another message giving our RON coordinates, which I radioed to the FOB. Just before it got dark, the indigenous team members crawled out and put claymore mines around our position. We then went to sleep.

ST Ohio, May 1968. Back Row: Sgt. John Barnatowicz with arms around Hlock and Het. Interpreter Nguyen Phung Tho standing right end. Mock 2nd from left middle row. (Robert Kotin photo)

I awoke sometime in the middle of the night and had to urinate. Before it got dark I had noticed that one of the indigenous team members was sleeping approximately eight feet to my left and slightly downhill from me. I also remembered there was an opening in the bamboo in the direction of my feet for about six feet. To avoid having my urine run downhill and onto the teammate to my left, I slowly got up and took three or four small steps into the bamboo opening and did my business.

Early in the morning, Kotin approached me and whispered, "Don't ever stand up at night in the RON. If we were over the fence, you would be dead because anyone standing in the RON at night is considered to be the enemy. If an RON has to be abandoned at night, you crawl out." I felt embarrassed at my first screw-up but was thankful that Kotin had warned me. I realized that there was a lot more to learn than I had anticipated.

I changed the round in the chamber of my CAR-15 when it got light, and Kotin coded up a message that included the direction of our intended travel. After we moved out for our second day, it started to rain, something we would have to contend with on each of the remaining days in the field. Being a medic, I carried some basic medical equipment such as hemostats to clamp off bleeders and a thermometer to check temperatures. On the third day of our mission Kotin complained of fever, and when I took his temperature it was 103 degrees plus. I gave him a chloroquine tablet to reduce his fever, assuming he was having a bout of malaria, a common occurrence. His temperature went down, but I could see he was still miserable as we conducted the rest of our mission. Day three and day four brought more rain, and at that point all of our gear was soaked. Kotin radioed a request to return to the FOB and on the morning of day five, permission was granted. He was still feeling ill as we made our way back to the compound.

When we got to the FOB, Kotin immediately went to the dispensary and I went to the mess hall for steak and eggs, a privilege extended to recon teams returning from missions. When I got back to the Ohio team room, someone stopped by and told me Kotin had a serious case of fever of unknown origin and was being sent to Pleiku for treatment. The following day I was advised he might be sent back to the States and that I would have to go to the debriefing to report on our exercise.

The debriefing session took all day, and it was during that session that I realized a mistake I'd made through inexperience. Kotin hadn't been writing a letter home, but was jotting down important notes about the mission. He had been observing and describing everything from the movement of the team to the size and diameter of trees and vines. I tried to piece his notes together the best I could, but my debriefing included a lot of guesses as answers to the questions I was asked. In the future, I would cut the daydreaming breaks and take my own notes on things that would likely be covered at the debriefings. I was glad that we had only been on a practice mission and not across the wire, as it was again evident to me how green I was.

I also began to fear that I would be moved into the One-Zero slot opened by the departure of Kotin. I didn't mention it to anyone, but I knew I certainly was not ready to take over the team. A couple of days later my fears were put to rest when I was informed that S.Sgt. Tommy Carr was being transferred to Ohio to fill the One-Zero slot. Carr had been the One-Two on ST Wyoming with One-Zero S.Sgt. Marshall D. Hall.

On May 18 and 19, Wyoming had been engaged in a two-day firefight with the NVA. Carr effectively communicated with supporting aircraft and directed airstrikes on the enemy forces. When the team was surrounded by enemy troops on three sides, Hall directed an artillery barrage on the enemy then led the team through the barrage, thus successfully escaping the encircling force.

The next morning, encountering a reinforced enemy squad, the team killed the point element. As Wyoming moved forward to search the bodies of the enemy, a renewed and intense counterattack drove them back. They held the NVA attacking force at bay for more than three

S.Sgt. Tommy Carr, ST Ohio One-Zero, July 1968. (Joe Parnar photo)

hours until they could be extracted. For their efforts, Carr would be awarded the Army Commendation Medal for Valor and Hall received the Bronze Star for Valor.

I met Tommy Carr in the club and we introduced ourselves to one another. He was one of the most arrogant people I have ever met and never missed letting anyone not airborne-qualified know that they were only legs. In the field, however, he was well disciplined and made few mistakes. He taught me important lessons such as selection of RON sites and the necessity of moving into these overnight positions only at last light. Also, Tommy loved to RON on steep hillsides where enemy sweeps of the area would be unlikely or so noisy as to give us opportunity to take defensive action.

As I got to know Carr better, he confided to me that he had not graduated from high school, but obtained his General Equivalency Diploma while in the service. He had read all of the classic works of literature that were required reading in college and possessed a wealth of knowledge on a variety of subjects. It was from discussions with Carr that I learned how the word "laser" was an acronym for light amplification stimulated by the emission of radiation, and that it was preceded by "maser" (microwave amplification stimulated by the emission of radiation). It was as if he was obsessed with reading and learning to make up for his initial lack of a high school diploma. Despite his arrogance toward legs, Carr was an excellent One-Zero and was good in the woods.

One of the things I had noticed after my first exposure to the jungle was the abundance of unusual plants and insects, the likes of which I had never seen back in Massachusetts. I had an insect collection when I was a boy and now wrote a letter home requesting my parents send me some insect pins, a pinning block, and a book on insect identification. I figured it would be neat to start a collection of bugs from Vietnam. I also asked that they send me a Buck General knife like one I had in Training Group that had been stolen. I liked it because of its unusually long blade, much longer that the combat knives issued by supply. And I asked them to send a Bob Dylan songbook I had at home so I could practice with the Gibson Country and Western guitar I bought from Gerry Denison when I roomed with him.

S.Sgt. Tommy Carr, ST Ohio One-Zero, and Sp4c. Joe Parnar ST Ohio One-Two, July–August 1968. (Joe Parnar photo)

Within 20 days the package arrived from home with my requested items. The bug collection never materialized because the first couple of beetles I pinned were destroyed when the team room maid moved the cigar box I was keeping them in and their legs and wings quickly broke off. My collecting had been limited to areas around the camp, since I figured Carr would probably shoot me if he knew I wasn't giving my full attention to the mission and was chasing bugs instead. I found the jungle to be beautiful and frequently thought how nice it would be to walk through it and not have to worry about being attacked by the enemy.

We trained for a couple of days with the team—going over immediate action drills to break contact and reacting to ambushes. After a couple more days Carr informed me that we would be going out on another practice walkout mission in the same area where Kotin and I had been. We drew our gear and made our final preparations.

CHAPTER 9

ST Ohio, July 1968—Second Mission

Tommy Carr was much more detailed in his instructions than Kotin. He was very specific on the gear he wanted me to carry and where he wanted me to carry it. One thing he was never without while running recon was a .45-caliber pistol worn in a shoulder holster. We went to downtown Kontum and he had me buy a similar holster from one of the Vietnamese shops. It had a small pocket on the outside for an extra magazine. I drew a .45 from supply at the FOB and a box of 50 cartridges.

Some of the gear I was to carry included the PRC-25 radio with extra battery, codebook, map, and a notebook and pencil. Also, each American carried an RT-10 emergency radio that was small and could be held in the hand. It enabled us to divert any aircraft flying in Vietnam and surrounding areas by coming up on "Guard" frequency and sending out a wide-ranging signal. When the aircraft responding got close enough, you could come up on voice and talk to the pilot. Rumor was that after getting an aircraft to respond, you had to establish verbal contact with the pilot or your location would be bombed under the assumption that the enemy was in possession of the radio.

The PRC-25 was carried in my rucksack with the handset wire extending out and under my left shoulder. I hung the handset on the web gear loop over my left breast so I could talk while holding the handset with my left hand and still grip my CAR-15 with my right. I wore a glove on my left hand to move "wait-a-minute" vines and other brambles out of the way and to avoid burns when the barrel of my weapon got hot.

Wait-a-minute vines were small, insidious trailing plants about ⅛th inch in diameter and several feet long with hook-shaped thorns that would stick into your clothing and gear. If you proceeded to walk through them, they would produce a loud ripping sound and tear or make runs in your rip-stop jungle fatigues. I quickly found the only sane way to deal with them was to take a half or a full step backward so they would disengage and then move them out of the way with a gloved hand before continuing.

Other signaling gear included a panel that was fluorescent orange on one side and red on the other. In addition, I carried two smoke grenades, strobe light, and a signal mirror. Tommy also carried handheld pen flares.

Ammunition and ordnance included the basic 22 magazines with 18 rounds of .223 CAR-15 ammo. We stuck tabs made from electrical tape on the bottom of the magazines so they could be pulled out of the tightly packed canteen covers that most recon men used to carry their ammunition. I put two boxes of unmagazined ammo in the bottom of my rucksack to save space and reduce the weight. I figured if I shot off all my ammo in a firefight, having to reload a couple of magazines would act as a reality check and make me conserve the remaining supply. In my CAR-15, I had two magazines taped together upside down so in a firefight I simply had to release the empty magazine then reverse and reinsert the full one.

Carr and I each carried six fragmentation grenades and I carried a "Willie Pete" (white phosphorous grenade) which could be used either as ordnance or for the purposes of signaling. I also had 14 rounds for my .45, but the only use I ever got from them in the field was to strip rounds from the extra magazine to toss at team members who snored at night in the RON. The downside of this was having to search and account for all the rounds when it got light.

Personal gear included a toothbrush that served to brush my teeth and clean my weapon. I carried four canteens of water, water purification tablets, insect and leech repellent, my Buck General knife, several combat dressings, gun oil, C-4 plastic explosive for heating water for coffee, my lensatic compass, a triangular bandana worn around the neck to wipe sweat, my small medical kit, and a minimum of food. I ran light on food and water since I couldn't get any other gear in my pack or on my web gear. The gear I toted, including my CAR-15, weighed 82 pounds when I placed it on the scale in supply.

The indigenous team members carried claymore mines, C-4 plastic explosive, and ammunition for the M-79 grenade launchers. In addition, we all carried 12-foot lengths of rappelling rope attached to the web gear and a couple of snap-links to fashion a Swiss seat for McGuire rig extractions. Carr also carried several toe popper anti-personnel mines designed to blow off a foot and deter trackers.

When we left the FOB on my second walkout practice mission, we took practically the same route I had with Kotin except we got farther up into the hills to the east of FOB2. As before, we experienced rain almost every day of the mission. On one of the mornings when I was changing the round in the chamber of my CAR-15, I found that the selector lever to take my weapon off safe was frozen. No one had mentioned to me that it was a good idea to move the selector off safe periodically during the day and add a few drops of oil to keep it from freezing up. I was again glad that we were on a practice mission as the situation would have been disastrous if we were over the wire and in a firefight. I had to disassemble the weapon to correct the problem. After this mission I always put adhesive tape from the dispensary over the muzzle of the weapon to keep dirt from getting in the barrel. I carried this practice over to my M-16 when flying chase medic later, and it paid dividends.

One luxury I enjoyed when in the field was a canteen cup of hot coffee. I got the coffee out of the C rations that were available to us. It came in small packets with accompanying packets of sugar and creamer. I would make a rectangular hole in the ground approximately four inches long, two inches deep, and one inch wide with my knife. Into it I put a one-inch-diameter ball of C-4 plastic explosive with a tail molded onto it that served as a wick. The C-4 looked like a cream-colored cherry bomb made of window putty. It burned with a yellow flame and an almost inaudible hiss and produced no smoke or odor. I placed a canteen cup of water over this mini slit trench and after about a minute would have a cup of water hot enough to make my coffee. I certainly looked forward to that cup of coffee each morning.

When we were well into the hills on the third day of the mission, we came upon a small hut built along the bank of a stream we were traveling up. We took written notes on the construction of the lean-to/hut and moved out once again. I saw that walking in the streambed eliminated footprints providing you made sure your steps were in the water or on rocks and not in the surrounding mud. I made mental notes of this and many other lessons Tommy was passing on to me. On day five, we made our way back by hitting the Dak Bla River and following it west until we came to the bridge north of FOB2 across from Kontum City and followed the road south to the compound.

Tommy and I were debriefed together, and this time it went much more smoothly. I was able to provide far more accurate input based on the notes I had taken. At least I was learning from my mistakes.

◊ ◊ ◊

A couple of days later Tommy returned from the morning One-Zero meeting and informed me that we had to dispose of some old mortar rounds and ordnance. He had drawn the detail because his primary MOS (military operational specialty) was engineer, which included demolitions. He directed me to get a couple of two-pound blocks of C-4 plastic explosive from supply and some det (detonation) cord and blasting caps. He also told me to get a case of grenades and M-79 rounds so we could practice with the team. He headed for the motor pool to check out a Deuce-and-a-half truck to take us to the 'Yard camp firing range roughly five kilometers south of the compound.

I went to supply and asked for the C-4. The American sergeant on duty advised me he would give me a whole case and said not to bring any back; I guess broken cases created paperwork problems. C-4 was always useful to have for cooking, and I didn't see a problem with accepting the excess. I was told the same thing regarding the det cord and given an entire coil of 150 feet. I met up with Tommy, and we loaded the truck and left for the 'Yard camp range with the entire team. I rode in the cab of the truck with Tommy, and the remainder of the team was in the open back along with the ordnance.

Aerial photo of 'Yard Camp. Camp is in center of photo east of highway QL/14 which runs north (L) to south (R) in this photo. Rifle range/demolitions area is to upper left of camp in cloud-shrouded area. (Paul Morris photo)

When we arrived, Tommy and I got out of the cab and climbed into the back. Tommy picked out a grenade and looked past the front of the cab. He noticed a crater about 25 feet in front of the Deuce-and-a-half that had been created when someone had set off a charge. It was approximately six feet in diameter, and the bottom was full of water from the almost daily rains. He pulled the pin and threw the grenade into the water-filled crater. The explosion sent up a waterspout nearly 25 feet into the air. He got another grenade, handed it to one of the Vietnamese on the team, and instructed him to do the same.

The Vietnamese team member pulled the grenade pin and threw the grenade over the cab and toward the water-filled crater. Not having baseball in their backgrounds like the American soldiers, the Vietnamese and Montagnards could not throw very far, and the grenade came up short and exploded five feet in front of the crater. We ducked our heads, and the blast made a couple of holes in the radiator of the truck.

I unloaded the case of grenades and began to twist off the wire sealing the hasp on the wooden case. Tommy said, "No, no, I'll show you how to do that." He took his .45-caliber pistol from his shoulder holster, angled it along the hasp, and then shot the hasp off the case.

I thought to myself, "This must be how you do it in a combat zone."

We proceeded to a berm at the back edge of the firing range and took turns tossing grenades. It quickly became even more obvious that the indigenous personnel could not throw them very far or accurately. I understood Tommy's reasoning when he now made it a rule that the indigenous members were not to carry white phosphorous grenades on missions. White phosphorous grenades were even larger and heavier than the egg-shaped hand grenades we had been throwing, and there was the distinct possibility of their burning team members if not thrown a distance of at least 15 meters.

We moved on to M-79 practice, and all took turns firing at a stump roughly 100 meters away. I came within five yards and was satisfied that I would have wounded anyone I was shooting at as the M-79 has a five-meter casualty radius. The last to fire was Mock, who put on a show for us. The M-79 was the weapon he carried on missions. Mock walked along as if he were on patrol with the target stump off his left shoulder. He dropped to his right knee and, as he was dropping, turned the M-79 to his left and fired from the hip. He hit the stump dead on. I figured it may have just been a lucky shot, so Tommy had him do it a second time. Once again, he hit the stump dead on, but he cut his knee when he dropped to the ground. I put a small dressing on the cut, having gained ultimate respect for Mock's proficiency with his weapon.

After completing grenade and M-79 practice, we turned our attention to the ordnance we were assigned to destroy. Tommy picked out another hole approximately five feet in diameter without water and we packed in the ordnance. There were both illumination and high-explosive mortar rounds, as well as grenades and trip flares. We next packed the case of C-4 so that it formed a crown over the top of the hole. Tommy then connected the C-4 blocks together with det cord. He ran the remainder of the det cord out about 150 feet and connected a blasting cap with

Rifle range/demolitions area at 'Yard Camp. Live fire immediate action drills and breaking ambushes training was conducted here. (Paul Morris photo)

90 seconds of time fuse and a pull-type fuse lighter. We loaded into the Deuce-and-a-half, then Tommy ignited the fuse lighter and we drove off.

We stopped almost a quarter-mile away to watch the fireworks. Several of the illumination mortar rounds went shooting off, with the initial explosion sending up an undulating mushroom cloud that looked like a mini atom bomb blast. As the mushroom cloud rose higher, it became a giant smoke ring. We all thought that was pretty spectacular.

The following day Tommy returned to the team room from a One-Zero meeting and informed me that a first lieutenant was taking over the team. To save the fellow embarrassment, I will only refer to him by his code name—"Rocky" or "Lieutenant Rocky." Somewhat surprised, we set off to meet our new One-Zero.

We found Rocky in his room and he immediately related several war tales of his bravery and heroism. I found this strange, as there was an unwritten rule followed by most recon men that you didn't brag about your own heroics. It was usually a teammate who told these stories, and new recon members generally kept their mouths shut until they had something to say. Rocky also said that he wanted Carr and me to help him move his gear into a new room he would be sharing with another officer. I never did learn why he wasn't moving into the Ohio team room. Once again, I thought this strange, as everyone I knew on recon moved his own gear. I shrugged it off as a privilege of rank.

A couple of days later, we were informed by Lieutenant Rocky that we would be going out on another walkout practice mission in the same area as my previous two. I was getting quite familiar with the area to the east of FOB2 by now. Part of our mission was to do a MEDCAP (medical civil action project) on a Montagnard village about two miles from the FOB. Reports were that there were several malaria cases in the village and we would be assisting in winning the hearts and minds of the villagers.

CHAPTER 10

ST/RT Ohio, July
1968—Third Mission

When we had assembled inside the compound for the mission, Rocky came up to me and asked, "Hey, Doc, what is the dosage on these pep pills?" He had some Green Hornets (capsules of 15 mg. dextroamphetamine sulfate that worked on a time delay) that recon One-Zeros sometimes carried in the event they had to stay awake at all costs. I explained to Rocky that they were not pep pills and had the unwanted side effect of allowing you to run your body into a state of physical exhaustion. When this occurred, your mind would want to perform an action, but your body would not be able to respond. I hoped the warning would suffice.

The first day was uneventful, and we RON'd on the same hillside that Tommy Carr and I had the previous week but in a slightly different area. Shortly after it got dark, I drifted off to sleep. Around 2300 hours I was awakened by Rocky, who informed me we had a killer team in our RON and one of the indigenous personnel was dead with his throat cut. He told me to contact the FOB, approximately a mile and a half away, and have illumination rounds from the 4.2 mortars fired over our heads. I switched on the radio and whispered into the handset, "Diamond Head, Diamond Head, this is Rocky, Rocky—Over."

Carr hissed at me from about eight feet away, "Shut that fucking radio off—and listen."

I shut the radio off and listened. I took out my Buck General knife and was ready to defend myself if anyone tried to cut my throat. But the only thing I heard was an occasional rustle as the indigenous personnel moved slightly. After a couple of hours I fell off into a frequently interrupted sleep.

When it got light, Rocky was looking on the ground all around our RON location, saying, "There would be tracks here if it hadn't rained last night."

I thought, "Where is our dead team member?" I then realized he had taken the Green Hornets and was hallucinating. Just what we needed was a drugged-up asshole team leader.

We continued on to the Plei Krako village and conducted the MEDCAP. If there had been malaria in the village, there were no signs of it now as no one had any high fevers. But many of the children had small cuts and bruises that had become infected. I gave several bars of soap and some antibiotics to the village chief. So as not to diminish the chief's importance and standing in the village, I had Tho tell everyone that the medications would only work if the chief himself dispersed them. After a couple of hours, we moved on to conduct our practice recon mission.

As we proceeded, Rocky became obsessed with the odd-looking termite mounds that were numerous in the area. He would approach them and start poking at the holes around the base. "They hide weapons under these things," he declared.

After a while it got embarrassing, especially when I saw Mock look at Het and tap his temple with his index finger, the Vietnamese sign for *dien cai dau* (pronounced "dinky-dow" by the Americans), meaning "crazy." At that point, I had lost all respect for Lieutenant Rocky and was embarrassed to be associated with him.

As we prepared to find an RON location for our second night, Carr told Rocky he would select a site that no one would sneak into after dark. Carr found the densest bamboo thicket in the vicinity, and we crawled and picked our way in. The bamboo was so thick that it required quietly clearing out an area in which to lie down. Carr and I began eating some rations and Rocky immediately fell asleep. As last light was failing, Rocky awoke screaming, "Aah! Aah!" and went crashing into the bamboo like a monkey. When he finally figured out he was dreaming, he sheepishly returned to where he had been and went back to sleep. I immediately realized that an action such as this over the fence in a hot area would be suicidal. I was fuming for the rest of the mission. It rained for most of the remainder of the operation, and day five we headed back to the FOB soaked.

After dropping my gear in the room, I headed for the mess hall for chow. On the way, Capt. Amado Gayol, the officer in charge of recon teams, approached me. Gayol was a Cuban who had been captured at the Bay of Pigs invasion. Word was that he had been ransomed from Cuba for some tractors. He told me, "Get your gear together. Rocky is taking out a Hatchet Platoon tomorrow to get some experience, and I want you to go along as the medic."

I responded, "Sir, I never want to go out with that man again."

He inquired why, and I explained all that had happened. He told me he would find someone else for the Hatchet Platoon. He asked me to tell Lieutenant Rocky that I couldn't go out because my gear was all wet rather than giving him the real reason. I proceeded to chow.

As I was returning to my room to unpack and dry out my gear, Rocky was crossing the road that divided the compound. He approached me and asked, "How come you're not coming out with me tomorrow? What's the matter, are you chicken?"

"Yes sir, I'm chicken," I said.

"No, I know you're not chicken, I saw how you conducted yourself out there. Why don't you want to go out with me?"

"Because my gear is wet."

He insisted that I give him another reason. I said that if I did so he would only get pissed off.

He replied, "No, I won't; tell me, tell me."

To this I responded, "Sir, I have absolutely no confidence in you as a recon One-Zero, and I think you are going to get people needlessly killed, and I don't want to be one of them."

"I suppose you think Staff Sergeant Carr behaved better?"

I could only answer that I thought Carr had acted a "damned lot better."

Tommy Carr was in the team room when I got back. I informed him of my conversation with Gayol. He said he already knew about it because Gayol had immediately come to see him after talking with me. He said he had corroborated everything I told Gayol. He also told Gayol that he was not going to say anything more regarding it because he figured the powers that be would only think it was a case of sour grapes due to his losing the One-Zero position to Rocky. Carr reiterated that he had confirmed that my report was what had actually happened.

I went to the showers to get cleaned up from the mission. As I was getting out of the shower, Gayol entered the area and lit into me.

"I thought I told you to tell Rocky your gear wasn't ready. How is he supposed to gain confidence if you tell him you don't have confidence in him?" I realized Rocky must have gone crying to Gayol following our conversation.

"First of all, Rocky would not take wet gear for an answer and demanded I give him the real reason. Secondly, this is not the place to come to gain confidence. If you don't have confidence in yourself to begin with, you shouldn't be here."

This really pissed off Gayol, and he told me I would regret it if I ever disobeyed another order from him. I kept my mouth shut but called him an asshole under my breath. I figured if I was willing to go out, risk my life, and die if necessary, then the officers in charge had an obligation to put competent One-Zeros in charge. I wasn't going to be silent about incompetent leadership that would piss away my life and the lives of others for the sake of their careers or experience. I also realized that I now had enemies among the FOB leadership.

Rocky went out with the Hatchet Platoon and came back with tales of enemy contact. His weapon had a bullet hole through the magazine well, which he claimed he got while he was rolling over a log. The problem was, he was the only one among the American or indigenous personnel who saw any signs of enemy contact. Furthermore, he did not have a magazine with a matching hole so he must have thrown the damaged magazine away, leaving good rounds for the enemy to police up. Speculation was that he had used one of the indigenous personnel's weapons to shoot a hole through his own magazine well, after having removed the magazine. In any event, the whole recon company was on to him and knew he was a phony.

Within a week word came down that Rocky was being transferred to CCN.

Recon teams party late July/early August 1968. Tommy Carr (left) with beer can in hand. S.Sgt. John Probart, dispensary supervisor, at cooler behind post in foreground. (Bryon Loucks photo)

There was a recon party held outside the recon team rooms along the south wall on the east side of the compound a day or two before Rocky was scheduled to depart, and he made the mistake of showing up. Tommy Carr was particularly caustic toward him and made a point of questioning him in front of everyone about why he was leaving us.

I kept clear since I knew I was already in trouble with Gayol and didn't want to press my luck. Carr later told me that he had said to Rocky that if he ever ran into him again, he was going to beat the shit out of him. Rocky left on the scheduled day, and Carr was put back in the One-Zero slot.

My worries regarding retribution from Gayol were allayed when he departed suddenly from the FOB a couple weeks later. I figured, however, that other officers were aware of the incident and might seek revenge. It made me apprehensive knowing that I would have people looking over my shoulder from that point on.

Around the time Gayol left, another NCO who had been involved in anti-Cuban operations disappeared from the FOB—a sergeant first class whose name was Ethyl Duffield. Duffield had arrived shortly after I got on recon, and everyone said he was present as one of the SF advisers when Che Guevara was captured and killed by the Bolivian government. I always had suspicions that he and Gayol were whisked away to work on some anti-Cuban, hush-hush project.

(It was only recently that I learned Sgt. Duffield was wounded and medevac'd on an operation on July 28 with 1st Lt. Michael M. McFall and Sfc. Walter M. Melton. My speculation all those years that he departed on anti-Cuban operations was apparently incorrect.)

CHAPTER 11

ST/RT Ohio, August 1968—Fourth Mission—West Near Plei Trap Valley

After Rocky's departure the team resumed training under Tommy Carr.

One of the critical skills needed by recon teams was rappelling-descending from a chopper by means of ropes and Swiss seats. He showed us how to rig the Swiss seat using our sling ropes. These were looped around the waist and tied off with the remaining ends looped around the legs and tied off again over the left hip. Gloves were worn to avoid rope burns. A snap-link was then connected to both tied-off systems and the rappelling rope looped through the snap-link. It was critical that the snap-link was attached to the Swiss seat correctly to prevent it from opening and disconnecting from the rappelling rope. Carr stressed this to the team through the interpreter, Tho. The left hand served as a guide above the snap-link and the right hand did the braking by moving the tailing rope down and to the rear, thus allowing friction on the right hip to slow the descent.

We each got to take two or three turns rappelling down the combination rappelling/water tower on the compound. The tower had a .50-caliber machine gun mounted at the top to help defend the compound should it be attacked. A steel pipe near the top edge represented a helicopter skid and was used to practice pushing off and dropping down far enough to avoid contact with the skid when exiting the aircraft. Carr also demonstrated a free rappelling technique that could be employed to descend cliffs, but it was useless for helicopter rappelling as one's feet needed to be in contact with something to keep from falling from the rope. I found this training to be among the most fun and useful of any that I underwent while on recon teams. I had always had a fear of heights and the adrenaline rush from the activity and the satisfaction of conquering my fear was exhilarating.

◊ ◊ ◊

A week or so after Rocky left, Carr returned from the One-Zero meeting and informed us we were going on our first real mission. The target area was approximately 20 kilometers southeast of the Plei Trap Valley, which lay to the west of FOB2 not far from the Cambodian border. It was north of the Dak Bla River after it flowed west then south past Kontum. We would be roughly 25 kilometers north-northeast of Plei

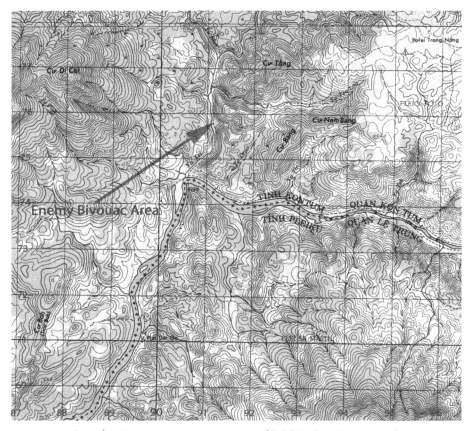

Fourth mission recon area to west of FOB2. (Joe Parnar map)

Djereng which had an artillery battery. Even though it wasn't actually "across the fence," we would be inserted by helicopter since the area was a considerable distance from Kontum. We drew gear for the mission and departed a couple of days later.

The LZ was a small clearing covered with chest-high brush. We had to jump nearly eight feet down into the brush, and I got my first taste of how difficult it was to determine exactly how far down the ground really was when the LZ was covered with vegetation. It seemed you would make contact with the ground when you least expected it and get a pretty good jarring.

We moved off the LZ, which was roughly a mile from the valley we were going to recon. We RON'd for the first night and, for the first time on a recon mission, I had to take a crap. Just before it got dark, I made my way out beyond the claymores, which the indigenous team members had set out, and I scraped out a hole with my Buck knife. I then dropped my pants and squatted over the hole with my CAR-15 lying on the ground to my left. I heard a noise behind me and turned my head and looked back to see Het standing guard over me while I crapped. I don't know whether he did it because he liked me or because he knew I was carrying the radio and my gear represented our ticket out if we got into trouble. I couldn't help but feel he was probably thinking "Stupid American."

That night I fell asleep at dusk but awoke shivering at about 2300 hours. I noticed that the vegetation around me was glowing in the dark. At first, I wondered whether the glowing was from some defoliant that had been sprayed but decided that since the vegetation in the area appeared healthy in the daylight, there was probably some other cause. In discussing this with other recon men back at the FOB after the mission, someone said it was due to some sort of mold or fungus that grew in the jungles. It did make the RON seem eerie. I had trouble sleeping the rest of the night and shivered from the damp and cold. I couldn't wait for it to get light so I could move and get some circulation going.

We ate at daybreak, retrieved the claymores, and moved out right after transmitting our morning situation report (sit-rep). By 0900 hours I was wishing it would get dark once again so we could stop and rest. The weight of my 80-pound-plus pack was pulling back on my shoulders and giving me a pain in my chest. It felt like my sternum was going to separate. My difficulties were probably the result of the fact that the hills in this area were considerably steeper than those encountered on my first three walkout missions. Periodic rain also made the hillsides slick, causing mud to cling to the soles of our jungle boots and add a couple of extra pounds to each foot. We would all occasionally slip and thus create unnecessary noise. When this happened, the rest of us would glare at the offending team member with eyes that said, "Keep quiet." Almost without exception, we each took a turn at being the offender. I cussed Carr under my breath as we moved exceedingly slowly and I always seemed to have to halt in mid-step, with one foot uphill and bent and the other one below with knee locked. This was a very uncomfortable position in which to remain, but it was necessary in order to maintain a proper interval between team members and avoid bunching up.

We RON'd on the side of a steep mountain where I learned another lesson. I decided to sleep situated up and down hill with my head at the high end. I braced my feet against a clump of bamboo and locked my knees to avoid sliding down. Once again, I slept until around 2300 hours and woke up not only cold and shivering, but also all scrunched up against the bamboo clump. In my sleep, my knees had unlocked and I slid down until my butt was resting on my heels. I raised myself with my elbows and inched back up to where I could lock my legs. My knees were sore and I found that even though I did not sleep again that night because of the cold, I kept sliding back into the scrunched-up position. I vowed that in future similar situations I would sleep horizontally on the hill and use the bamboo clump to keep me from rolling downhill. It was another long night of shivering and wishing it would get light.

In the morning, Carr gave me a coded message to relay to Covey. In transmitting the message, I drew a blank when I got to the letter "Q." Tommy chastised me and I practiced running through the phonetic alphabet used by the military. At daybreak that same morning, I got to hear my first monkeys. They started whooping, first at a low pitch that rose with each whoop and then got more frequent. The whoops would build to a high-pitched crescendo until abruptly dropping off with a descending "whoop." While this was going on, Carr made a motion suggesting the monkeys were jerking off and the fading "whoop" meant that they had shot their load. He indicated this by smiling and hanging out his tongue as if in bliss. I laughed to myself, but figured he was probably right as the sounds fit his mime act perfectly.

Day three meant more humping up and down mountains. During one of our breaks, Mock sat near a clump of bamboo and was staring intently into it. He looked up at me and pointed to my Buck General knife on my web belt. I took out the knife and tossed it to him. He leaned into the clump of bamboo and after a short rustling noise came out with a small, venomous green snake minus its head. One of the Vietnamese near him motioned for Mock to give the headless snake to him. This fellow put the flame of his lighter to the headless stump of the bamboo viper, causing it to recoil like a spring. The actions brought smiles and giggles from the rest of the onlooking Vietnamese team members. As I was lying back on my rucksack in some long grass, I thought to myself, "I hope there isn't a nest of those little buggers around here." I was so tired from carrying the radio that I decided that even if there were, I would let them bite me. I was too exhausted to move to a new position.

Later in the day we came off the hillside and descended into a small valley with a stream running through the bottom. We emerged from the thick hillside vegetation right where an enemy bivouac area was located. There were three shelters built of bamboo and roofed with banana leaves. Each was about 20 feet long and 10 feet wide with no walls. It looked as if a company-sized unit could probably fit under them to sleep. We also found a grave on the eastern edge of the complex. We took notes on the structures and radioed our discovery to the FOB. As we waited for a reply, I checked one of the sleeping shelters more carefully. There were some empty C-ration cans that had been left behind, so I picked one up and sniffed it. There was no odor, which indicated to me that it had not been there very long. My guess was that a unit of NVA had spent the previous night here and moved out at first light after eating.

The instructions we received from the FOB directed us to cross the stream and proceed west up the mountain. When we were clear of the area, we were to call in artillery from the American firebase at Plei Djereng.

We moved up the mountainside for the rest of the day until stopping to call in the artillery. We were approximately two kilometers from the bivouac area at that time. Carr walked me through the proper procedure for calling in artillery. After firing a couple of marking rounds, I gave the order to "fire for effect." Somewhere in my mind, I kind of expected the whole valley to go up in flames and explosions, like in the World War I or World War II movies, but I was in for a big disappointment. The shelling came in three-round salvos with maybe a minute in between. We could hear the impact in the valley below us roughly a mile away. We had no way of knowing how accurate the fire was, only that it was landing somewhere in the vicinity of the location of the bivouac area. About 21 artillery rounds were discharged during the fire mission. I was a little disappointed that Hollywood seemed to have better artillery than the military.

Carr found an RON location near the area where we had called in the artillery strike. That night Het had a high fever of around 104 degrees. I gave him some chloroquine, suspecting that he had malaria and was experiencing an attack. The medication reduced the fever, but I could see that he was still feeling poorly.

In the morning we called in our morning sit-rep, and Carr requested to be extracted because of the ill Montagnard. We received instructions to return to the enemy bivouac area and do an artillery damage assessment. We were also instructed to dig up the grave to see if it was an enemy cache. I didn't relish the thought of hiking over a mile back down into the valley, but orders were orders.

It was around noon when we reached the bivouac area. The artillery had slightly damaged a couple of the shelters, but with a little repair they would be good as new. Carr set some demolition charges on all the structures, and we proceeded to dig up the grave. When we dug down a couple of feet, it became obvious that we were not breaking into an enemy cache, but exhuming a dead body. The smell was putrid and I immediately stopped breathing through my nose. We departed the area after pulling the fuse lighters on the charges Carr had set.

We headed back up the mountainside via the same route as the day before. We heard the charges go off to our rear and continued on, searching for an LZ for extraction. The FOB had agreed to this only after getting us to do the artillery damage assessment. It seemed every request made to the powers that be generated a conditional reply.

By mid-afternoon we were halfway back up the mountainside when Covey appeared overhead. We were directed to an LZ, which was in an area where 12-foot-high elephant grass was growing. We began to clear an opening by extending both arms from our sides, falling down backward, and laying the elephant grass down flat. After each lay down, I dragged myself back to my feet for the next effort. I realized just how tired I was. On my last lay down, something started burning on my left eyelid. I then saw things buzzing around my eyes. Despite my fatigue I jumped to my feet and ran across the cleared portion of the LZ while brushing at my left cheek. It quickly became evident that I had fallen back into a hornets' nest. My eye began to swell, and after 10 minutes I couldn't open it or see out of it.

By now Carr decided we had cleared a large enough area for the helicopters to land in. All that remained was to get rid of a 10-foot tree stump right in the middle of the LZ. Carr strapped a claymore around it and strung out the firing wire to its limit. He detonated the mine and neatly cut off the stump at ground level. Fifteen minutes later the choppers arrived and extracted the team.

Joe Parnar with swollen left eye from hornet sting while clearing extraction LZ. (Joe Parnar photo)

The steak and eggs tasted especially good back at the FOB, and for the first time I felt we really deserved it. We had encountered recent enemy presence and successfully destroyed a bivouac area. I just knew it wouldn't be long before we drew a real mission across the fence.

◊ ◊ ◊

A couple of days after this, probably the most embarrassing incident that happened to me during my time in Vietnam occurred.

When I got up in the morning, my footlocker was all wet. I was looking at it puzzled, and Carr told me I had gotten up in the middle of the night and was stumbling around the room in the dark. When he heard the sound of splashing water, he told me, "Joe, go outside and piss." He said I responded, "I am outside," so he let me finish. I had no memory of being awake but was extremely ashamed about the incident.

After mission—Mock and Joe Parnar posing with weapons and gear. (Joe Parnar photo)

My footlocker had a crack along the top and all the clothes within were soaked with urine. I wonder what the Vietnamese maid thought when she had to wash my clothes that day? I was thankful Carr never brought it up in the club to add to my embarrassment. I guess the stress of recon was present in ways in which I was not conscious.

◊ ◊ ◊

It was after this mission that the Vietnamese team members gave me a gift. Amid much snickering and giggling, they presented me with a pair of black pajamas. I couldn't figure out if they were telling me that my soldiering skills were more beneficial to the Vietcong or that the pajamas

Carr (right) and Parnar (left) after mission four. (Joe Parnar photo)

were for women. I never did get what the joke was. The pajamas were not jungle-worthy and looked to be made for a leech feast. I thanked them for the gift and figured maybe it was payback for the case of Cokes I sprung for after each of our first four missions.

A few days later during stand-down, Carr came into the room late in the afternoon and told me to get my rucksack, web gear, and weapon. He said the helicopters were available to practice exfiltration by McGuire rig. I had been drinking all afternoon and had already consumed six to eight beers. We would not be using Swiss seats since the ropes that dropped down from the chopper had a web loop that went around the waist and a couple of leg loops that were attached to the ends of the ropes. Four of us were going to be hoisted up at a time.

When we were lifted off the ground during the exercise, the waist loop caught under the canteen pouches on my web gear, which carried magazines for my weapon. My weight, plus the weight of all my gear, pushed the canteen pouches into my diaphragm and was suffocating me. I also felt as if I was going to barf from all the beer I had drunk and shower those clustered below me. When we were about a thousand feet up and circling the FOB while dangling from the ropes, I finally wiggled enough so the waist loop slid up under my armpits and I was able to breathe. After that experience, I never looked forward to being pulled out by strings on a mission. Before this, whenever I was flying chase and had watched other teams being extracted by this method, I always thought being strung out on a McGuire rig looked like fun.

Once again, reality was brought sharply into focus.

◊ ◊ ◊

On August 23, we lost 1st Lt. Paul D. Potter. He was our S-4 officer in charge of supply at FOB2 and had gone to CCN for promotion board. A sapper squad infiltrated the compound that night and killed 17 Americans. As far as lives lost, it was the costliest day in the history of Special Forces.

CHAPTER 12

Promotion Board

We were waiting for our next mission when Carr returned to the room one morning from the One-Zero meeting and advised me that the two of us were being flown to Nha Trang for promotion board. We immediately made our way to the chopper pad and caught our flight. We landed in Ban Me Thuot on the way for refueling, then continued on to SF headquarters at Nha Trang.

Upon our arrival at the 5th Group headquarters, I was approached by a sergeant major who chewed me out because the flash on my beret was dirty. He ordered me to go to supply and get a new one. We then checked into the transient barracks. Along with Carr and me, Adrian Zadick, another FOB2 recon team member, was to attend the board.

The next morning, we reported for the promotion board. It now occurred to me that I had not had a haircut or trimmed my mustache for some time. I slicked my hair down the best I could and tried to trim my mustache by biting off the scraggly hairs that would reach far enough into my mouth.

First, Carr went before the board by himself, and afterward Zadick and I were called in together. The officers on the board asked Zadick who was running for vice president of the United States for the Republican Party in the upcoming election. Zadick replied, "I don't know," to that question and to most of their other questions.

They then asked me who was running for vice president of the United States for the Republican Party in the upcoming election, and I correctly responded, "Spiro Agnew."

I continued to answer their questions and was feeling pretty good about the proceedings until being cross-examined by the only sergeant major on the board. His question to me was "Specialist Parnar, what is your definition of neat and trimmed?"

I hesitated to answer since I was not sure he was referring to my hair or my mustache. He rescued me a short time later by saying, "I am referring to your mustache. Do you think your mustache is neatly trimmed?"

To this I responded, "No, sergeant major."

"Weren't you read a directive by your commanding officer stating that anyone who comes onto this SFOB will have a neatly trimmed mustache if he has one at all?"

"No, sergeant major."

He then asked Zadick if he had been read the directive to which he responded, "No, sergeant major."

This ended our appearance before the promotion board.

◊ ◊ ◊

Zadick and I met Carr outside the building. Tommy said since it was payday, we could draw a partial pay while we were here instead of waiting until we got back to FOB2. That way we could at least have some fun. We drew our pay and headed downtown for a night of partying. Each of us got into various forms of mischief, and we split up with the dates we had arranged for at one of the bars. I woke up somewhere in Nha Trang the next morning in the house of one of the bar girls. I walked down several streets until I got my bearings and hitched a ride back to the SFOB.

Later in the day, back at the transient barracks, Zadick, Carr and I swapped tales of the previous night.

That evening, we went to the NCO club where they were having a floorshow with strippers. At the NCO club, we met up with several people from CCN whom we knew and greeted our comrades with a wet French kiss in the ear. We were quickly informed that this practice was not tolerated in the NCO club. Of course, this made us repeat it at every opportunity just to piss off those in charge. Eventually, I was caught in the act and escorted out of the club by two bouncers. When we arrived at the door, the people at my table were already there, and while the bouncers were trying to push me out, my friends were pushing me back in. Finally, the bouncers, being stronger, or maybe more sober, prevailed. We exited like an exploding zit and ended up on the ground. I jumped up and pulled out my .45 pistol, ready to go back in and shoot the bouncers. Carr told me to forget it and we headed back to the transient barracks since we would be leaving the next day. As we passed in front of the orderly room at headquarters, I asked Carr for permission to fire my weapon.

"Make yourself happy," he said.

I fired off two or three rounds into the ground, and we made our way toward the transient barracks.

When I awoke the next morning, sober but hung over, I cringed at what I had done. I couldn't wait to leave and figured that if we stayed in Nha Trang another day, we would all be in jail. We departed later in the afternoon and returned to the FOB, where we learned we were not being promoted. I didn't particularly care, as I didn't have any intentions of making a career of the service and had already realized that the pay would have sucked even with the promotion. When I finally did get promoted five months later, my pay with all the goodies—separate rations, overseas pay, combat pay, jump pay—amounted to the equivalent of an entry-level salary for someone with no high school education in civilian life.

CHAPTER 13

ST/RT Ohio, September 1968—Fifth Mission

A couple of days after return from promotion board, Carr informed me we were getting another American on the team. The new man was S.Sgt. Luke Dove, whom we met later that morning. His arrival meant that I would be graduating to the One-One position and would no longer be carrying the PRC-25 radio.

We went to the PX and Tommy and I each got a case of beer to celebrate. I had started drinking beer at about 1000 hours in the morning and didn't stop until 0100 hours the next morning when I passed out while reading a *Time* magazine on my bunk. I believe this was the most beer I ever consumed in a 24-hour period, and I awoke with a monstrous hangover. Carr also said that I owed him a half case of beer. I asked why, and he told me I had drunk my case plus half of his. My estimate was that I must have had 40 to 50 beers the previous day, counting the ones I consumed at the club that night.

We trained with Dove for the next couple of days. Something that especially concerned Carr was the enemy probing our RON location at night. One morning he said that he had obtained some old grenades and wanted us to practice silently activating them. We did this by pulling the pin, easing off the spoon—which produced only a pop—and lobbing them after a count of two. A weapon zeroing pit had been scooped out with a bulldozer just outside the wire surrounding the compound off the south wall. With the daily rains, it was full of water, and we sat on the mound to the rear of the hole and practiced the activating procedure. The grenades sent up 20 to 30-foot waterspouts, which added to the fun.

S.Sgt. Luke Dove, RT Ohio One-Two, August 1968. (Luke Dove photo)

On a couple of occasions, the grenades were duds and did not explode. When subsequent grenades were thrown in and exploded close enough to the duds, it caused secondary explosions with two waterspouts per grenade. While we were enjoying ourselves, one of the FOB officers appeared on the south wall of the compound and yelled, "What the hell are you doing?"

Carr yelled back, "We're disposing of some old grenades." The officer just shook his head and left.

◊ ◊ ◊

The next day Carr advised us the team had drawn another mission and would be doing a recon of the local area to the south of the 'Yard camp. On mission day our team was trucked to the starting point just east of the highway to Pleiku, a few miles beyond the 'Yard camp.

We quickly slipped into the jungle and immediately came upon a stream that drained off the mountain area we were going to check out. Traveling up the streambed made our movements much easier, but it was on this mission that I got my first introduction to another element of jungle operations.

In the wet area near the stream, leeches abounded. When we stopped for our first break there were probably a half-dozen of them on each of my boots, worming around and trying to find a way in. Back in the States, after getting orders for Vietnam, I had nightmares about leeches. Snakes were never a concern to me, but the thought of leeches crawling over me and sucking out my blood made my skin crawl. I felt uneasy until I received my first bite. When we stopped for one of our breaks, I noticed a wet spot on the calf area of my jungle fatigue pants. The cuff had become slightly un-bloused, and I pulled up the pant leg. On my calf was a leech, full of blood. It had drunk its fill and was no longer attached to my calf, but there was a hole where it had been that was oozing blood. I picked off the leech and doused it with the greasy leech repellent I carried. I realized that I had not even felt it when I was bitten, so from that time on I would rather a leech bite me than a mosquito. Mosquito bites itched and carried the potential of malaria.

We RON'd away from the streambed so we wouldn't have any more leeches crawling over us. A common but eerie occurrence that night in the jungle was the presence of Tokay geckos, which we called "fuck you" lizards. This was because they would produce a sound that sounded exactly like someone saying "fuck you" over and over. The sound was so clear and distinct that you would swear that it was a person cussing at you outside your RON.

The next day we moved up the mountainside that was now becoming more of a steep hill. As we approached the top, we were called to a halt when the point man encountered an American trip flare. We proceeded to the top of the hill, which had a large rock outcropping at the summit. It looked as if an American unit had set up a defensive perimeter on this hilltop sometime in the recent past. We found several more trip flares attached to trees, and Het and Tommy Carr disarmed a couple of them. We assembled near the rock outcropping where Tommy gave me a lesson on how to dispose of the trip flares. Holding down the metal spoon with one hand and pulling the pin with the other, he then tossed the flare away from him. It immediately ignited with a pop while leaving his hand, and the blinding white magnesium flame followed.

Next it was my turn. I held the spoon down with my left hand and proceeded to pull the pin, but the flare ignited in my hand with a pop even though I was still holding down the spoon. I immediately flung the burning flare away from me but got splattered by burning magnesium in the open "V" area of my shirt near my neck and chest. I burned my thumb, and a hardened pad formed as a result. It was as if the heat was so intense that it had cooked the first two layers of skin and formed what looked like a callus. It throbbed like hell but never blistered. I also saw a white spot in my vision for the next couple of hours from the brightness of the magnesium flame. I learned a lesson not to mess with trip flares. In the future, if I ever had to disarm any, I would pull the trip wires and let them burn out on the trees where they were mounted.

Carr directed us over the mountain, and we found a road on the other side. He radioed for an extraction, and we were picked up by a truck sent from the FOB. It was an uneventful mission, but we got to see some pretty country and it gave the new One-Two, Luke Dove, his first experience in the jungle. I believe the mountaintop with rock outcropping was Hill 1126, approximately three kilometers southwest of Hill 1152, to which the radio relay site "Sledgehammer" was moved after it was abandoned from the mountaintop overlooking the Plei Trap Valley. Following the move, it was renamed "Klondike."

One of the surprising things about being on recon was that my eczema improved vastly whenever I was in the field on operations. I would have thought that with the heat and unsanitary conditions I experienced in the jungle, my condition would have been aggravated. Erythromycin effectively controlled any infection that would come up, but I think not taking a daily shower was the reason for the improvement. Infrequent showers let the dried body fluid form scabs and allowed time for the skin underneath to heal over. Daily showering, instead, washed away the scabs and exposed the fresh, skinless areas to renewed weeping.

CHAPTER 14

ST/RT Ohio, September 1968— Sixth Mission—Camp Perimeter Recon

A few days after returning from the local area recon to the south of the 'Yard camp, Tommy Carr said the team had been assigned the nightly recon around the perimeter of the camp to the east of the compound. He told me he wanted me to take the patrol out to gain experience being a One-Zero. Dove would carry the radio, and we would take the indigenous team members with us. The nightly perimeter recons were run by two separate teams to determine if there were any enemy in the immediate area. One team ran the perimeter to the east side and one to the west side of the north–south highway that divided the compound. The missions entailed moving one to two kilometers out and making a semicircular arc around the camp.

We left the compound via the north gate and turned right, following the same route I had traveled during my first three walkout missions. After we passed through the Montagnard village near the compound, we began veering southeast to begin our swing around the eastern perimeter. We were about a half-mile from the FOB when we heard a single shot, then a short time later, a second one. They sounded to be roughly 500 meters distant from our location. I had Dove radio the FOB to inform them that we were hearing shots. The reply came back to go and investigate their source.

I called Tho over to me and told him, "We go catch them." He relayed the instructions to the point man and before I knew it, the point man took off running in the direction of the shots. The rest of the team followed and left me waving my arms trying to stop them. In my instructions, I had assumed they would know I wanted them to proceed with caution. I now learned yet another lesson—don't assume anything! I began running after the team, trying to get them to stop. All I could picture was the NVA or VC firing a few single shots to draw us into an ambush. The entire team was strung out for about 100 meters and proper interval between members was not being maintained.

When I finally did catch up to the point man, he had captured the person who was doing the shooting. It was an old Montagnard out hunting with a U.S. carbine. His shirt was stuffed full of small birds, most likely for his supper. He said to Tho that he was a part of the CIDG (Civilian Irregular Defense Group). I had Dove radio the FOB that we had apprehended the individual responsible for the shots. They told us to bring him back for questioning. I felt bad for the old 'Yard since it was obvious to me that he was only trying to get supper for himself and his family. I took the team aside and tried to explain through Tho the dangers inherent in what they had just done by not staying together and proceeding with caution.

We returned to the FOB with our prisoner. We left him with the S-2 (intelligence) staff and headed back to the team room. I rated my performance on this mission extremely low, as it was obvious to me that I had lost control of the team. I wished I had said that we were to "slowly" investigate the source of the shots. I realized that stressing such details when giving instructions to the interpreter was paramount. I told Carr about the incident, but he didn't seem overly concerned despite the fact that it really bothered me.

A couple of days later I was informed that I was being pulled off recon. I then recalled that I had been on recon for nearly three months and figured that the powers that be had not forgotten that I had been taken out of the dispensary when Pappy Webb got me on Team Texas. The pieces began to fall into place and I knew that Team Ohio had only gotten a third American because he was to be my replacement. My feelings were a bit hurt, but I didn't complain too loudly. By this time, the glamour of recon was gone. With a half-dozen missions behind me, even though they were practice missions in Vietnam, I appreciated how grueling and physically demanding recon operations actually were.

I rather looked forward to riding on a helicopter again in support of those operations instead of humping an 80-pound rucksack up and down mountains. The experience of being in the jungle on recon, however, would serve me well on future operations with the Hatchet Force. I knew how to act when in the field, and running recon had taught me to avoid doing anything stupid. From one standpoint, my experience had probably been a waste. I was trained and almost ready for missions across the fence, but now that training would not be put to use. And Team Ohio was back to having an inexperienced One-One once again.

I reported to the dispensary the following day. I immediately went back into the rotation of working there some days and flying chase medic on others. Even though I was no longer on recon, I had a real appreciation of what the teams on the ground were going through as we orbited high above in support of their missions.

One of the new medics that had come on board while I was on recon was S.Sgt. Anthony Dorff. Tony had been in charge of the 7th Group Dispensary when I worked there after training group before my orders for Vietnam came down.

Tommy Carr and Luke Dove moved to a new team room. Then Dove transferred to RT Delaware and was replaced on Ohio by S.Sgt. David L. Warrum. Not long after that, Carr, Warrum, and RT Ohio went on TDY (temporary duty) to Ho Ngoc Tao near Saigon for a few weeks. When they returned, Carr was ready to DEROS and the team seemed to disband. Mock and Hlock were picked up by RT New Hampshire, and Dove brought Het over to Delaware. Tho went to RT Florida as the interpreter.

A few days after Carr and Dove moved out, Ralph Rodd, One-Zero, and Ken Worthley, One-Two, of RT Florida moved in with me. They were the only two Americans on Florida at that time, so I was instructed to remain in the room. I roomed with Ralph and Ken for the next couple of months.

CHAPTER 15

Back to Chase Medic

Shortly after getting back into the chase medic rotation, I was sent to Dak
To on Bright Light standby with a Hatchet Platoon of Montagnards. A
recon team was operating in a hot area, and the FOB expected trouble
and wanted to have us ready, just in case. It was five days of boring duty
waiting around Dak To all day. We bivouacked at the site of the former
Special Forces camp that had been bulldozed flat with the exception of
a two-story, concrete bunker-like building that served as our command
post. I camped out with the Montagnards in the rubble in a small tent
made of two shelter halves. I collected some boards and laid them down
so I wouldn't be sleeping in the mud if it rained. Someone else had
brought a bunch of paperbacks, and I spent my days reading. We ate C
rations all during this time, and I developed a heightened appreciation
for the quality of the meals we were served back at FOB2.

On one of the days, the Montagnards went down to the river to the
south of the airstrip to swim and get cleaned up. They came back with
a huge carp that came floating up when one of them threw a grenade in
the water. The fish must have been nearly three feet long and weighed
30 to 40 pounds. The 'Yards made quite a feast of it that evening.

The recon team in the field never got into any serious trouble and
was safely extracted. The 'Yards and I were choppered back to FOB2
and I returned to the dispensary.

While I was on recon, a fulltime Bright Light presence at Dak To was
established, with a recon team pulling five days of continuous duty and
staying there overnight. Once when I was flying chase, RT Texas was

on Bright Light standby at Dak To, and I was talking to Pappy Webb. Pappy told me that in 1967 a whole company of the 173rd Airborne Brigade had been wiped out on the big mountain just across the river to our south. It would not be for another 25 years that I would learn that Tom Deschenes, my friend from AIT and jump school, was with that company and had been killed during the battle. Had I known it at the time, I would have taken more notice as Pappy pointed out the mountain.

◊ ◊ ◊

When I reported to the dispensary in the morning on another one of my chase medic days, Bill Lensch gave me four body bags to take with me. RT Colorado had found an unidentified helicopter parked in the jungle with four corpses nearby. I was supposed to go in and remove them. My chopper pilot had to cut down some small bamboo stalks with the rotor blades before getting to the ground in a very small opening in the jungle. At first, I thought the cracking of the bamboo was AK-47 fire being directed at us, but none of the crew seemed concerned.

After we had landed the Colorado One-Zero, Sgt. Dennis Mack, came up to our helicopter and handed me a poncho tied off at the top.

I asked him, "Is this all there is?"

He nodded, then turned and returned to his team to continue their mission. When we cleared the trees, I opened the poncho and found four skulls, a couple of femurs, and a few other assorted bones. Word came to us a few days later that the skulls were all Asian and no Caucasians appeared to have been among the bodies found in the vicinity of the mysterious helicopter.

◊ ◊ ◊

My chase medic duties over the next month to month and a half were not noteworthy. On days that I was working in the dispensary, however, significant events were taking place. On October 5, Gerald Denison, aka Grommet, was called upon to fly Covey Rider support for a recon team that had been split up and was in enemy contact. He reported for his briefing at 0630 hours and shortly thereafter met one of the 219th Aviation Company SPAF (Sneaky Pete Air Force) pilots at the Kontum airstrip. They flew to Laos to the team's last known location where they spotted two or three individuals flashing emergency panels.

As they expanded their search, they made a turn up a small ravine or valley and began taking .51-caliber machine gun fire complete with green tracers. The pilot banked hard left to clear the top of the ridge but struck the top of a large teak tree. This occurred at 0725 hours and Grommet had recollections of bouncing off every branch on the tree from top to bottom as the Bird Dog was going down. He doesn't recall who the Covey Pilot and Rider were that subsequently arrived on the scene and coordinated their rescue, but the helicopter assets were based in Kontum, and most likely were from the 57th AHC.

Grommet was visited at the 71st Evacuation Hospital at Pleiku by Paul Poole who told him he looked like "a Rembrandt painting with such pretty colors—red, yellow, and purple." He had suffered extensive injuries, including lacerations and cuts to the tendons on three fingers of his left hand, and had a hole in his left shoulder caused by an enemy round or a piece of the aircraft. A foreign object had gone through his left cheek, fracturing his upper jaw in three places and the lower in five, and he lost a number of teeth. He still sports a four-inch scar on his left cheek as a reminder of the events of that day.

Thus, on October 5, 1968, FOB2 lost one of its greatest assets and most skilled Covey Riders. Gerald Dennison's calming and reassuring voice coming over the radio to teams in a crisis on the ground was to be greatly missed.

After being stabilized in Pleiku, Grommet was sent to Camp Zama, Japan and from there to Fort Dix, NJ and then on to Valley Forge General Hospital. His recovery took over a year before he was released to full duty. He later returned to CCC in 1971, only to be medevac'd after the Covey shack was hit by a 122mm rocket, wounding him a second time.

◊ ◊ ◊

During my time at FOB2, there were very few formations in which we were provided information in a formal manner. We had periodic formations that we were required to attend, but these were generally only awards presentation ceremonies.

The most valuable information was to be obtained while sitting around tables in the club after hours, listening to stories told by recon team members of their experiences on recent missions. Everyone paid close attention to these stories in order to find something out that might be of value in the future. Since there was no television at the FOB, these sessions served both as entertainment and as informal classes on lessons to be learned. Most of the accounts were presented in a humorous style, over beers, and no one really bragged about his exploits. If someone did do something heroic, it was one of his teammates who would relate it. This was typically preceded by an introduction such as, "You know what that stupid shit did?"

Our only other entertainment at the FOB were the nightly movies shown in the theater just outside the club, and an occasional floor show. We saw some good films, like the Clint Eastwood spaghetti Westerns, and that is where I first saw *The Green Berets* starring John Wayne. Some of my friends in Medic training had met him at Fort Bragg during the making of the movie.

Often, the antics in the theater were as entertaining as the action on the screen. One night we learned that one of the NCO's had shot a civilian cow that had been wandering outside the wire. Since the FOB had to pay for the cow, they were trying to find the identity of the culprit. The individual responsible was said to be missing his right index, or trigger, finger. Paul Poole commented in the theater, "I don't know who shot that cow, but he pulls the trigger like this," and indicated pulling the trigger with his middle finger.

One time someone farted and asked me, "Hey, Doc, do farts have lumps?" I should have presented him with a bill for medical consultation.

On another occasion, Kontum City was getting hit with mortar fire while we were watching a movie. Heads craned to the right and to the left to look around the screen and see the rounds exploding in the city. We could even hear the rounds leaving the mortar tubes somewhere in the distance. The film never stopped, though, and we never even had an alert at the FOB as the city was on the other side of the Dak Bla River. It was like watching a movie and the war at the same time.

During our many discussions in the club, it was frequently mentioned that the CIA was conducting similar missions to ours much deeper in Laos. Somehow, after seeing the James Bond movies, I figured that these people drove around in Aston Martins with mounted machine guns, had beautiful babes on each arm, and were paid hundreds of thousands of dollars. It wasn't until I was out of the service that I learned the CIA didn't pay all that much more than the military. Apparently, the CIA relied on their agents' patriotism the same way the military did ours.

◊ ◊ ◊

One of the best friends I made during my tour with SOG was a fellow medic by the name of Ronald Brown. Ron was a Native American, a full-blooded Navajo, whose family lived on the Navajo reservation in New Mexico. His mailing address was Two Gray Hills Trading Post, Tohatchi, New Mexico. He was the first Native American I had ever known. I had had a keen interest in Indians ever since I was a small boy and listened to a radio show called *Straight Arrow*, whose hero was the son of a Comanche warrior. The sponsor was Nabisco Shredded Wheat, and they used to put 4x7-inch cards in their cereal boxes to separate the layers of the shredded wheat cakes. These Straight Arrow "Injun-Uities" cards had information printed on them explaining how the Indians crafted many of the items they used, such as their shields and weapons and canoes. My mother, after always telling me I could be anything I wanted to be when I grew up, had quite a difficult time trying to explain to me why I couldn't be an Indian.

The name Ron Brown was given to him by the government school he had to attend. His name in Navajo was, phonetically, to the best I can attempt, "Esh-Kay-Ho-Lich." I asked Ron on many occasions to pronounce his name and I would try to say it, but each time he informed me I wasn't doing it correctly. I guess my mom was right.

Ron used to request that they play "The Ballad of Ira Hayes" by Johnny Cash on the stereo in the club, over and over. Ira Hayes was the Native American Marine who was awarded the Presidential Unit Citation for helping raise the flag on Iwo Jima during World War II. Someone finally destroyed the copy of that record so they wouldn't have to listen to it any more.

Sgt. Ronald Brown, medic. (Bryon
Loucks photo)

Around the time I was getting off recon, Ron was flying a chase
mission and his helicopter was pulling a team out using McGuire rigs.
While the crew was lying on the floor of the craft and attempting
to lower the ropes and direct the pilots, Brown saw an NVA soldier
firing at the chopper. Since I knew him quite well, I asked Ron for
the details. He said the NVA would peek out from behind a tree, take
a couple shots, and hide behind the tree again. Ron jumped into one
of the crewmembers' seats and got behind his M-60 machine gun. He
waited until the NVA peeked out once more and then drilled him.
Brown acted like what he did was nothing, but the Huey crewmembers
thought it significant enough to write him up for an Air Medal for
Valor, which he was awarded. (A medal with "V" meant that someone
had distinguished himself in combat as opposed to simple achievement
or meritorious service.)

In January 1969, a reinforced platoon from the 'Yard Camp was
conducting a reconnaissance in force operation in Target Area Hotel-9
to locate a truck park that was suspected to be in the area. The unit was
led by Captain Ronald Goulet accompanied by Sergeant Brown who
was serving a dual role as platoon medic and squad leader. Ron would
receive a Bronze Star for his actions while on the mission. He remarked
that he was really impressed by the leadership abilities of Captain Goulet

on the operation. Ron was also wounded in early March 1969 and received a Purple Heart.

It has never ceased to amaze me how Native Americans fought so bravely for the United States, especially after the way our government had treated their people in the past. Ron Brown was one of the finest people I met in the service, and I have always regarded him as a brother.

I also became good friends with Ralph Rodd and Ken Worthley after they moved into the RT Ohio team room when Carr and Dove moved out. Rodd was one of the most gung-ho One-Zeros I ever met. I don't think he bothered to take leave or R&R at all in his first year in Vietnam, preferring to go out on missions instead. I believe he ran a total of 26 missions during that time. Some were in Vietnam, but the majority were across the border. Worthley was what I would describe as an "all-American boy." Unlike most of us, he never resorted to vulgarity to express himself; he probably was confident enough so that he did not have to resort to crude talk to make others think he was brave and tough. Long before I ever communicated with his mother, I knew what an outstanding family she had raised by the actions and deeds of her son.

Sgt. Ralph R. Rodd, RT Florida One-Zero. (Craig Davis photo)

Sp4c. Kenneth W. Worthley, RT Florida One-Two, fall 1968. He later became RT Florida One-Zero and was KIA on 26 August, 1969. (Joe Parnar photo)

During one of our rap sessions in the club, Rodd related how his team had jumped a tiger on one of their missions. Another time, while his team was checking out a structure in the jungle, the inhabitants' pigs came up to them and started grunting. The friendly pigs were just being curious. Rodd tried to make them go away as they were drawing unwanted attention to the team.

Rodd also told me that once when RT Florida was about to launch on a mission, a reporter tried to get on the chopper with them. Rodd had to kick him off. Shortly after that, as I was flying over Laos, I thought how any reporter in Vietnam would probably give his left arm to sit where I was sitting at that moment.

By early 1969, Rodd's circle of friends had all acquired a taste for the PIRs (prepared indigenous rations) formulated for use by SOG by Ben Baker of the Counter Insurgency Support Office (CISO). The PIR rations, referred to by SOG personnel as "indigenous rations," were freeze-dried ingredients such as shrimp, green beans, and hot peppers for seasoning. After the club would close, Rodd frequently hosted rice parties where indigenous rations were prepared in a large ammo can using C-4 to heat up the mixture. These late-night meals were enjoyed by all and really hit the spot.

Baker and CISO worked to develop equipment and other items required by the unique nature of SOG. One such item was the SOG Bowie knife used by many soldiers on recon. Eldest Son and Italian Green—the booby-trapped AK-47 and mortar ammo we planted in enemy caches—were also creations of CISO. At one point, Rodd was training his point man to fire an AK-47 so he could carry it with him on missions. He hoped that it might give his man an edge if an enemy momentarily held his fire upon seeing another soldier dressed like he was and carrying the same type of weapon. Unfortunately, one day Rodd had to bring his point man into the dispensary so we could sew up a gash on his head. The weapon had exploded and the bolt blew out, hitting him in the head. Apparently, the AK-47 ammo he got from supply had one of the Eldest Son rounds mixed in with the good AK ammo.

On an in-country mission, one of the indigenous team members of RT Florida was wounded during an encounter. Ralph called in air strikes onto the opposing force's position, but after a brief battle, the opposition was identified as friendlies. Someone had not done their homework, as neither friendly force was aware the other was conducting a mission in the area. Both sides took casualties. Another example of the fog of war.

Sfc. William L. Kendall was strap-hanging with RT Florida on October mission when Tho lost his foot. (William Kendall photo)

Another significant incident in which I was not involved took place on October 14, 1968. Rodd had previously picked up Tho as the interpreter for team Florida after RT Ohio disbanded upon returning from Ho Ngoc Tao. On the 14th, he was putting together an improvised team consisting of Sfc. William L. Kendall as One-One, and acting One-Two Sgt. Larry Briggs, for a bomb damage assessment mission into Laos after a B-52 arc light. Kendall and Briggs were strap hanging to gain recon experience, and Worthley did not accompany Florida on this mission.

The team was checking out some tunnels in the arc lighted area when Tho jumped into the entrance of one of the tunnels and picked up a wire. Both Rodd and Kendall yelled and tried to stop him but it was too late and an explosion blew off Tho's right foot. They administered morphine and called for an immediate medevac. After approximately two hours they were extracted and Tho went to the hospital for treatment and rehabilitation.

I didn't learn of the incident until 1969 when Rodd brought Tho into the dispensary inquiring about getting an artificial leg for him. For the most part, the Americans on recon were very concerned with the well-being of their indigenous teammates and Rodd was no exception.

(Tho lived in Kontum not far from the FOB after the war. He passed away from cancer in January 2016. I talked to him on the phone on a couple of occasions prior to his passing.)

Nguyen Phung Tho was hired as interpreter of RT Florida after RT Ohio disbanded upon returning from Ho Ngoc Tao. (Robert Kotin photo)

Tho being carried by teammates shortly after losing his lower leg and foot. (Larry Briggs photo)

◊ ◊ ◊

While I was living with Rodd and Worthley, we decided to request an extension of our tours in Vietnam. I was concerned that after DEROS I would have to go back to Fort Bragg for the remaining four months of my enlistment. I figured it would be four months of spit and polish and chicken-shit details, and preferred to spend my time in Vietnam. In early December, our requests were denied, with the proviso that an extension would be granted if we agreed to serve for another six months in Vietnam. This would have pushed my ETS (elapsed time in service—the date you are discharged from the service) out another two months. Because I never had any intentions of making a career of the Army, I let the denial stand. Rodd and Worthley, however, resubmitted their requests and agreed to the additional time. After his extension period, Rodd even re-enlisted and became a career Special Forces soldier. Worthley was later KIA in August 1969 in Cambodia during his extension.

◊ ◊ ◊

Another recon One-Zero for whom I gained great respect was Joe Walker, code name "Gladiator," who was the One-Zero of RT California. Joe was famous for volunteering for missions in the hottest targets. On one occasion, a recon team took several wounded when their RON location was hit with RPGs. Joe volunteered to go into the target area about a week later. He had experimented with firing a 60mm mortar while using a sling over his shoulder and was going to carry it on the mission.

S.Sgt Joe J. Walker, RT California One-Zero with California Republic banner. (Joe Walker photo)

Joe Walker before hand–firing 60mm mortar with strap around neck. (Joe Walker photo)

I remember him stating that he was hoping the NVA would attack his team in their RON because he would have a surprise for them.

Another time, I was flying chase medic when we extracted Walker's team following a prisoner snatch attempt in Laos. RT California had set up for an ambush alongside a bend in a jungle trail. When an NVA appeared, someone on the team shot him in the legs with a silenced weapon. Before they could run out and secure the prisoner, a second NVA came around the bend. Joe's Montagnards panicked and then

Joe Walker after firing 60mm mortar. (Joe Walker photo)

started firing and blew away both enemy soldiers. Later on, following their extraction, Joe took the team aside at the holding area at Dak To and, like a football coach in the locker room after a bad game, proceeded to chew them out.

The two NVA had been carrying American made M-16s and Joe brought these back along with their gear, plus every stitch of clothing they were wearing. When I asked him why he did this, he responded, "When they debrief me, if they want to know how many buttons were on the NVA's shirts, they can count them themselves." Walker recalls turning in the captured weapons, uniforms, clothing, and equipment to S.Sgt. Thomas Sheridan at the mission debriefing.

Many recon men thought some of the debriefers' questions bordered on the ridiculous.

◊ ◊ ◊

There were several accidents involving weapons at the FOB during my tour. On one occasion a helicopter pilot accidentally shot himself in the calf while checking his weapon after getting out of his helicopter. Another time, one of the NCOs had his .45-caliber pistol go off in his shoulder holster, and he shot himself in the hip. A third accident resulted when an American brought his Swedish K into the club. One of the 4th Division personnel who was also in the club asked him about the weapon, and the recon team member said, "It's a Swedish K," and fired from the open bolt position. Another recon team member took the weapon in order to continue this demonstration. He accidentally fired off a burst of rounds and struck two people sitting at a table when two of the rounds ricocheted off the floor. Paul Morris, with whom I had served on RT Texas, was one of the people hit, taking a bullet that traveled from the bottom through the top of his foot. The person sitting at the table with Paul was hit in the calf. Paul was sent to Japan for a month to recuperate.

Even the club could be a dangerous place.

◊ ◊ ◊

Early one evening, I was in my room when I heard a single shot from the area of the Texas team room. Several of us rushed over there to find out what had happened and to see if someone had accidentally been wounded.

Pappy Webb had two new Americans on his team, and one of them had purchased a small green parrot while down in Kontum City. He made a small perch for the bird on Pappy's table in the team room, where he was keeping it as a pet. Personally, I think Pappy was pissed off that the parrot was always shitting on his table and scattering seeds everywhere. When we entered the room, Pappy was putting his .45 back into his shoulder holster. Someone asked him what happened.

"I've just had a firefight with the parrot," Pappy replied.

There were blood and feathers all over and around the table. Someone else later said Pappy told him that when he stuck his finger near the parrot, it bit him, so he shot it.

Though we had pulled out several teams under fire, there were no KIAs at FOB2 during the month of October.

CHAPTER 16

SOG SLAM VII—Medic Assigned to SLAM Company

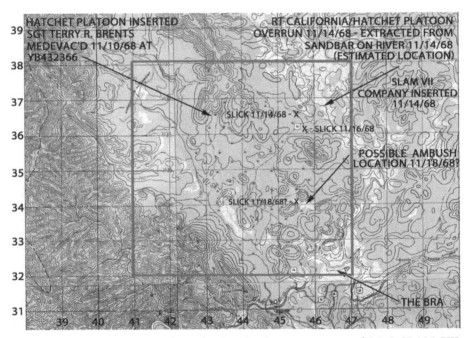

Target area Juliett 9 and significant landmarks depicting events of SOG SLAM VII, November 10–19, 1968. X's mark locations of downed helicopters. Locations ID'd by Captain Gary Higgins of 361st Aerial Weapons Company (aka the Pink Panthers). (Joe Parnar map)

I was flying chase medic on November 10, 1968, the day S.Sgt. Joe Walker's team, RT California, was operating in target area Juliett 9, north of the Bra in Southern Laos along Highway 96. A Hatchet Platoon

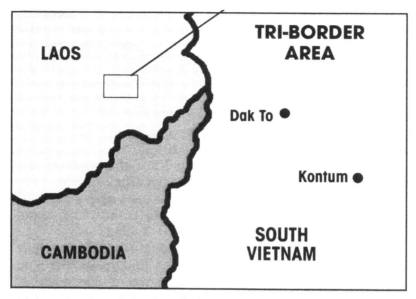

Map with inset showing relationship of Juliett 9 and tri-border junction. (From original edition of *SOG Medic* by Paladin Press)

from Company C (Montagnard) led by 1st Lt. Lee Swain had already been inserted and linked up with Walker's team. I rode on a chopper that was going to extract a wounded American, Joe's One-One, Sgt. Terry Brents. It took two trips into the LZ to locate and pick up the wounded team member.

The first time we entered the LZ there was no one in sight. My initial thought was that we might be in the wrong location and I was looking around puzzled. I caught the door gunner's eye and mouthed, "Where are they?"

He just shrugged his shoulders and held his palms up to indicate he didn't know. We then left the LZ and gained altitude, orbited a short time, and went down again. I wasn't sure if we had returned to the original landing zone or a different one as I was scanning for signs of the team or enemy movement. When we touched down, we could finally see members of the team about 30 meters off to the side.

I jumped off the chopper and met several Montagnards and an American who led me along what seemed to be a pathway to Joe

1st Lt. Lee R. Swain and Hatchet Platoon Montagnard. (Lee Swain photo)

Walker and his wounded team member, Sergeant Brents. Every five meters a Montagnard was posted to guard the path. Brents had a head wound, but his pulse was strong and he didn't appear to be in too much distress. I also remember Lieutenant Swain, the commander of the Hatchet Platoon, being on the scene. Joe Walker told me they had encountered NVA with boards mounted on their chests from which grenades were hanging so they could throw them two at a time. We brought the wounded American to the chopper and flew him back to the 4th Division medical facility at Dak To where he was treated. Brents would survive his wounds. Meanwhile, Walker's recon team and Swain's Hatchet Platoon embarked on a joint mission.

Later that evening, I was sitting in the club when Ralph Rodd came in and told me that Captain Lesesne was telling everyone a story that a chase medic would not get off the helicopter to pick up a wounded American. This was pure bullshit. I hurried over to Lesesne's office and walked in without knocking. With the relaxed restrictions on saluting officers at the FOB, I had forgotten protocol. He was sitting at his desk and I said, "What is this shit you're spreading about me not getting off the helicopter?"

I must have caught him by surprise because for five seconds or so he just sat there. Finally, he realized he was a captain and I was only a specialist four, because he responded, "What do you mean coming in here and reporting to me like that?"

I snapped to attention, saluted, and said, "Sir, Specialist Four Parnar reports."

He then let me speak. I explained that the first time in the LZ there were no friendlies in sight and the door gunner didn't know where they were when I asked him. I told Captain Lesesne that the second time in, after we identified friendlies on the LZ, I did get off the chopper and helped bring Brents back to the ship. I informed him he could verify this with Swain and with Joe Walker when they got back from their mission. I left his office but would still bear a lot of animosity toward Captain Lesesne for long while afterward. I suspected this all might be retribution for the incident with Lieutenant Rocky and Captain Gayol when I was on recon the previous summer.

◊ ◊ ◊

A couple of days after the Hatchet Platoon was inserted and Brents was extracted, one of the Americans, S.Sgt. Joel Haynes, twisted his knee and needed to be medevac'd. He was replaced by Sp5c. Floyd Bryant. This occurred on the 12th or possibly the 13th while RT California and the Hatchet Platoon were continuing to operate jointly.

On the morning of November 14, I went into the dispensary to see where I would be assigned that day. Sgt. Bill Lensch informed me that the recon team and the Hatchet Platoon had been overrun the night before and that a SLAM Company was going to be inserted to relieve RT California and get out the dead and wounded. He said the SLAM Company did not have a medic assigned to it so one of us would have to cover. He asked me if I had my gear ready to go, and I replied I did. While flying chase, I always had my medic's bag ready. He told me to never mind the briefing that was going on at that moment and just get my gear and report to the choppers as they were almost ready to leave.

The SLAM Company was to be led by Captain Lolly Sciriaev, who spoke English with what sounded to me like a Russian accent. He was new at FOB2 and no one seemed to know much about him. Because of the size of the company, around a hundred men, it was going to take two separate flights of the eight helicopters—four Huey slicks and four Kingbees—to make the insertion. I was among the first half of the company to be flown to the Dak To launch site. We waited there for more than an hour for the choppers to return to Kontum to get the second half of the company. Four helicopter gunships waited with us at Dak To. Finally, after everyone had arrived at Dak To, the first half of the company launched for insertion into Juliett 9.

I went in with the first group, but on the fourth or fifth chopper. The landing zone was a sandbar on a river, approximately 20 meters wide. We got off the choppers and sought cover along the north bank of the river. The last two choppers coming in drew 37mm antiaircraft fire from what seemed like a considerable distance to the southwest.

Sandbar (center) on river north of the Bra that flowed south into the Dak Xou. Insertion sandbar for SOG SLAM VII Company on November 14, 1968. (Image © 2015 Digital Globe, Google Earth Point satellite photo, January 10, 2006)

On the hillside across the river was the RON site where RT California and the Hatchet Platoon had been overrun the previous night.

I met Joe Walker near the sandbar. He had a couple of the Montagnards from his team with him that had reunited after scattering the night before. He had received fragment wounds but refused my offer to look at them, saying he was all right. One of the lenses of his glasses had been blown out during the attack, and I wondered how he could make sense of anything with one eye fuzzy and one seeing clearly.

I did not know it at the time, but the air assets had been busy prior to the launch of the SLAM Company, medevac'ing the seriously wounded from the Hatchet Platoon and RT California. One of the choppers carrying wounded was shot down and crashed about a kilometer southwest of our insertion sandbar. On board was Walker's One-Two, S.Sgt. Rudolph Machata, who had been wounded in the night-time attack. After the medevac chopper crashed, he organized the wounded

S.Sgt. Rudolph G. Machata, RT California One-Two, November 1968. Later KIA at CCS in 1969. (Rita Machata photo)

and helicopter crew and planted charges on the downed bird to destroy it. Machata then led the wounded along with the pilots and crew back to the sandbar through enemy-controlled terrain. His actions would earn him an Army Commendation Medal for Valor.

While we waited for the helicopters to return to Dak To and bring the second half of the company I talked to Joe Walker. I mentioned my concern that if anyone was still alive at the RON site, they probably needed medical attention ASAP. Joe agreed and said, "I'm going up there."

He took one of his Montagnards, went to Captain Sciriaev, the SLAM Company commander, informed him he was going back to the RON site, and led the way. Sfc. Bob Howard, Lieutenant Swain, and a few others also volunteered to go, and I tagged along as the medic. I remember Bob helping some of the small Montagnards across the river as the water was quite deep. He held them up with his arms since the water would have been up to their eyes.

Sfc. Robert L. Howard (left) and Sgt. Ernest Moreland (right) in 1968. (Craig Davis photo)

We proceeded up the hillside when the word came down that there was someone who had been found alive. I worked my way up to the RON site. There were five dead indigenous personnel in and around the perimeter of foxholes that had been dug the previous night. I was directed to a depression where I found a severely wounded black soldier. It was Sp5c. Floyd Bryant. He was conscious, and I reassured him that he was going to be all right and began assessing his wounds. I opened his jungle fatigue shirt and there was a pool of nearly a quart of blood with large clots formed in it. I knew he was in shock and needed replacement fluids, so I started an IV and plugged in my only 1,000cc bottle of Ringer's lactate. I was fortunate and hit the vein on the first try. I then proceeded to bandage and dress his wounds. My pack generally contained a bottle of Ringer's, three cans of plasma, an adrenaline kit, and 40 to 50 combat dressings of varying sizes, as well as miscellaneous items like hemostats, bandage scissors, tape and morphine. When I had finished dressing Bryant's wounds, I had used almost half my dressings. He had about 19 wounds over his body.

As I was applying the dressings, he told me a chilling tale. He said after sunrise the NVA came through the site and shot the dead and wounded. One of them shot him in the head, but he just played dead. He had two small wounds on his forehead with what looked like a black and blue streak running under the skin connecting them. One wound was where the round had entered. After traveling a short distance under the skin, it had exited at the site of the second wound.

While I dressed Bryant's wounds, others prepared a stretcher from two bamboo poles and a poncho. Four soldiers carried the litter and I shuffled alongside holding up the IV bottle. When we crossed the river, there was a helicopter on the sandbar waiting for the wounded NCO. Bill Lensch was onboard, so I knew I was putting Bryant into capable hands.

I then took cover on the east bank of the river while another chopper came in to remove the dead and to medevac Joe Walker and the rest of the wounded. While we were retrieving Bryant and the dead bodies from the RON site, the balance of the SLAM Company had been inserted. I assumed at this point that our mission was over and we would be extracted soon. Was I ever wrong.

Something else I did not realize was that I was not the only medic assigned to accompany the SLAM. Tony Dorff was also there, having been inserted while we were recovering Bryant and the dead bodies. I never saw Dorff at the time, however, since the company was somewhat spread out and we did not move about socializing.

I wished now I had attended the briefing because it was becoming evident there was more to this mission than just pulling out the dead and wounded. After approximately an hour we received instructions to proceed in the direction of the 37mm guns that had been shooting at the choppers. I realized I had screwed up royally as my chase medic pack contained only medical supplies but not any food. I mentioned this to no one though. I felt it was due to my own lack of foresight that I had not brought anything to eat and nobody else should suffer for it. I resigned myself to the fact that I would be without food for the balance of whatever our mission was going to be.

We headed south, following the river for about a half mile, and crossed it by wading through rapids where the water was waist deep. I remember clearly how exposed I felt crossing the river, praying no one would open fire on us. If firing did occur, hitting the dirt, or in this case water, or even crouching down, would have resulted in being swept down the rapids. But we made it safely and traveled another 200 meters and prepared to RON. Hours later during the night we heard a dozen trucks or so to our west, probably on Highway 96. As I remember it, the Montagnards had not dug foxholes that night, but it didn't matter as we did not get hit.

The next morning, after most of the company had eaten and was preparing to move out, one of the American NCOs came over to me and offered me half of an unfinished spaghetti LRRP ration, which I accepted. Apparently, he had been watching me and noticed I had gone off by myself and was not eating. We then moved out for our second day in Juliett 9.

The day went without incident. I remember passing what I thought were drop-off fuel tanks from a plane; or perhaps they were napalm or CBU (cluster bomb unit) canisters. We walked most of the day and prepared to RON on a small hilltop. This time the Montagnards dug

Sp5c. Stephen M. Roche, Hatchet Force, November 1968. (Cliff Bottemiller photo)

foxholes around the perimeter. I selected a place for the night near Sp5c. Steve Roche and Bob Howard. I knew Bob had already been awarded a Distinguished Service Cross and had an impeccable combat record. I figured if anyone would know what to do if we got hit, it was Howard, and I felt more secure being near his area.

None of the Americans dug in but instead picked spots to sleep on open ground. Steve Roche either was told I had no food or figured it out on his own. He offered me a can of C rations, which I once again accepted. Before dark, I looked around for the nearest cover to crawl to in case we got hit and found an old rotted tree stump and log. Steve Roche let me sleep alongside him and shared his poncho liner to try to keep us both warm.

I was jolted out of a shallow sleep at around 0400 hours by an explosion, followed by another. Steve asked, "What was that?"

I said, "We're getting hit!" and began crawling in the darkness toward where I remembered the cover to be.

When I got there, I found the place already occupied by three other people; apparently everyone in that immediate area had selected the same safe haven the night before. Bob Howard and I were the last in the group to get there. An explosion from near where Steve and I had been sleeping hit Bob and me in the back with fragments.

Bob Howard proved why my reasons for wanting to be near him were well founded. He now crawled away from our group and began directing the Montagnards to fire their M-79 grenade launchers, but not their rifles, so the muzzle flashes would not be as obvious. After another five minutes of incoming rifle grenade and possibly RPG fire and outgoing M-79s, the enemy broke off their attack as suddenly as they had started it. I then proceeded around the perimeter to check on the wounded.

There was a total of 11 wounded who in my estimation needed to be medevac'd. Although none of the injuries were immediately life threatening, I was concerned about the high possibility of secondary infections. Among those wounded in the night attack were Sgt. Jon Davidson and S.Sgt. Bob Van Hall. Also wounded was 1st Lt. William Groves. Groves had been treated by medic Tony Dorff who himself was wounded. All of them were needing to be medevac'd.

After tending to the wounded, I found myself near where the radio operator and Captain Sciriaev were. I remember someone commenting that air support had been requested more than half an hour ago but

1st Lt. William J. Groves—wounded during attack of November 16, 1968. (William Groves photo)

S.Sgt. Anthony C. Dorff— medic wounded during attack of November 16, 1968. (Tony Dorff photo)

Sgt. Jon P. Davidson—wounded during attack of November 16, 1968. (Jon Davidson photo)

S.Sgt. Robert L. Van Hall, Jr.—wounded during attack of November 16, 1968. (Joe Parnar photo)

nothing was in sight yet. We had been told the day before that there would be a "Spooky" C47 gunship with mini-guns on station for us that night.

About the time it was getting light, the air finally arrived and laid down strikes all around us with no return enemy fire. Shortly afterward, some choppers were supposed to be coming in to medevac the wounded.

I was sitting back at the spot where Steve and I had been sleeping and noted that a rifle grenade had exploded approximately three feet from where our heads would have been had we not crawled for cover.

One of the company officers came by and motioned for all of us to gather around him. He said Captain Sciriaev, as well as himself, and all the other Americans he had talked to, felt our mission was now compromised since the enemy knew exactly where we were and had us surrounded. This could have been true, as we had been hit from all sides of our RON position. He then asked us for our opinion, and we all agreed that the enemy knew where we were, so we probably were compromised. I was amazed at how democratic combat really was. I didn't speak up because I didn't even know what our mission was and thought we had accomplished it when we got out the remnants of RT California and the Hatchet Platoon two days previous. The officer said that if everyone agreed, after he completed his rounds, Captain Sciriaev would radio the FOB and request an extraction.

A half-hour later, I again made my way around our perimeter to where the wounded were waiting to be medevac'd. I took a position near the SLAM commander. All of the officers were advising him to radio back and tell the FOB we had to be extracted because we were surrounded and would be wiped out.

I asked one of the wounded Americans waiting for medevac what was happening, and he told me the response to the original request for extraction was, "Break out of your encirclement and continue your mission."

This was getting interesting, so I hung around to see what would be the outcome of our second request for extraction. The next message

1st Lt. Craig Collier, 57th AHC, in his Huey, 1968. (Craig Collier photo)

relieved Captain Sciriaev of command of the SLAM operation and put the second in command, a first lieutenant, in charge. With the message were orders for the captain to get on board the first medevac ship, along with the wounded. I felt bad for him because all of the other officers had pushed for him to request an extraction the second time.

The medevac helicopters then arrived. The evacuation of the wounded was conducted by the 57th AHC based out of Kontum airfield. One of the pilots, 1st Lt. Craig Collier, recalled picking up an officer called "Little Hawk" whom he had also medevac'd back on October 27. Little Hawk was the code name of 1st Lt. Groves. Both times Collier had picked Groves up, he was wounded and bloody.

It was now apparent to everyone that our mission was not being directed by the commander on the ground, but micro-managed by FOB2, Saigon, or possibly powers above that. Prior to this we had been told the decisions of those in charge in the field, recon One-Zeroes or Hatchet Platoon or SLAM commanders, would not be second guessed by those at the bases. Either we had either been misinformed or the policy had changed. And once Captain Sciriaev got on board the chopper, I never saw him again at the FOB.

◊ ◊ ◊

The new SLAM commander, 1st Lt. Thomas W. Jaeger, immediately called for air strikes just beyond our western perimeter, and we moved out heading west. Our progress was slow, and I was positioned about three-quarters of the way to the rear of our single column. After traveling approximately 200 meters, we stopped for a while, and I could hear more air strikes being called in to our west and southwest. We continued on for another 100 meters or so until hitting a well-used, tire-marked dirt road—Highway 96. The column turned south and began walking the road. Our advance was still slow as the new commander was having some SPADs drop cluster bombs ahead of us. Tree limbs, branches, and leaves now littered the road. We had walked one-eighth to one-quarter of a mile south when we stopped again for 10 minutes before continuing.

After another 100 meters we came to a field telephone right in the middle of the road with a round ball of rice sitting on top. The wires attached to the telephone extended down the road in the same direction we were headed and disappeared around a curve. A bunker that could hold two men comfortably had been built into the banking on the west side of the road. Evidently, this was where our commander decided we should change directions, because the column was now veering to the southeast and back into the jungle. As I passed the telephone, I overheard 1st Lt. Price discussing with another officer whether to take the telephone, and whether to plant some Italian Green (booby-trapped) mortar ammo we were carrying in the bunker. I never knew what their decision was or whether we took the telephone.

After heading into the jungle for about a quarter-mile, we came to an area where some really neat foxholes had been dug. There were enough of them to easily accommodate our entire company. I remember someone suggesting that we RON in those foxholes, but then someone else pointed out that if Charlie dug them, he could probably lay rifle grenades in them all night long. We moved on and finally stopped to RON after another quarter-mile.

That night Steve Roche and I borrowed an entrenching tool from one of the Montagnards after he had finished digging his foxhole. I don't know how those 'Yards did it. The best Steve and I could do was to scrape out a shallow depression that wouldn't even hold one of us. The ground was like a rock.

I had run out of cigarettes after our second day. I quickly became adept at taking breaks near an American with cigarettes and looking at him like a sick puppy while he lit up. It usually resulted in an offer of a smoke. At this point, everyone was running low as some of the men had gotten their cigarettes soaked when we crossed the river the first day. I remember one American had broken open all of his wet cigarettes and wrapped the tobacco in a sheet of paper. Every break he would sit down near a spot where the sun hit the ground, open up the paper, and let the sun dry out the tobacco. I don't know if he had rolling papers with him or was going to use pages from his notebook.

The night passed without incident. In the morning it was apparent that everyone was running low on food and water, as well as cigarettes. This led me to suspect that this mission was being planned as we went along. I conjectured that the 37mm antiaircraft guns offered us an objective that could not be quickly moved out of our way, so if we kept moving toward them the enemy would eventually have to stand and fight. By pulling out the platoon and inserting the company without incident, it gave the FOB command fresh troops in enemy territory and a known fixed target of opportunity, provided we continued southwest toward the guns. This remains conjecture to this day because I was not part of the debriefing afterward and never did learn if we actually had a mission or what it may have been. One thing I did know was that we were zigzagging, but generally heading in the direction of the guns.

On day four, November 17, we passed an open area and word came down the line that we would be resupplied. We proceeded a few hundred meters and came to another open area where we stopped and set up a hasty perimeter along one side of the clearing. The open area was approximately 100 meters long and 50 meters wide. This would be our LZ for resupply. A message now came down the line that two bundles would be dropped by parachute and there would be a mortar in the resupply. We talked among ourselves that we had enough shit to lug without carrying a mortar, base plate, and ammunition.

Once again, Craig Collier of the 57th AHC, was supporting our mission and it was his helicopter that would drop the supplies. The chopper made its pass and we watched the first bundle dropped disappear into the trees a half-mile away. A second bundle was then dropped and landed in the jungle about 100 meters from our perimeter, so some of the men went out to retrieve it. A short time later, we heard a single shot from the vicinity of where the first bundle had landed and figured the NVA had found it.

(Years later Collier apologized for not getting that first bundle to us but also admitted that the chopper crews had never practiced dropping bundles to troops on the ground and had no idea at what particular altitude and airspeed to kick them out. The SF troops on board the helicopter apparently didn't know when to kick out the bundles either.)

The detail returned with the second bundle. It was a wooden case marked "mortar ammunition." Someone commented, "Great, we've got the mortar ammunition to lug along and Charlie has the mortar." When the case was opened it was filled with cartons of cigarettes. I got five full packs of Marlboros. This resupply was better than food, water, or ammunition. I remember how the first cigarette I lit up made me dizzy from not having smoked for so long. Evidently, someone's code name for cigarettes was "mortar ammunition."

We were still running low on water and food and continued another quarter-mile where we set up a perimeter around another clearing so we could finish being resupplied. The opening was more or less the same size as the previous one, and a chopper came in and dumped a bunch of things, including food and water. The water was packed in plastic bags six inches in diameter and five feet long. I was told to help carry some of the supplies off one end of the LZ to where we would RON for the night. The RON location was about 100 meters off the LZ and up a gentle slope.

We were dropping off the supplies when gunfire broke out on the LZ. Some of the men in our group were told to set up a defensive perimeter at the newly selected RON site, and then we received word by squad radio that someone on the LZ had been hit. 1st Lt. Price's platoon had been left on the LZ until the resupply was finished and the NVA had shot one of his Montagnards. A small group of us led by 1st Lt. Walter Huczko, Jr., made our way back there. I followed Bob Howard down the hill. As we got within sight of the LZ, the wounded 'Yard ran from the center of the clearing where the supplies had been dumped, toward where Howard and our small relief column had stopped. Seeing him out in the open, I said, "Let's give him some cover," and started shooting into the brush to our right flank.

After my initial burst Bob told me, "Good idea," and joined me in shooting until the wounded man was off the LZ.

The Montagnard had taken an AK round through the elbow and Price had put a tourniquet around his arm. I applied a pressure dressing to stop the bleeding and removed the tourniquet that had been hastily applied. To my surprise, the bleeding remained stopped with just the pressure dressing. I figured the wound, though it would undoubtedly cause him disability for the rest of his life, did not warrant his losing his entire arm. I would save the tourniquet as a last resort. With darkness approaching it was apparent we would not get him medevac'd until the following day. I then put his arm in a sling made from a triangular bandage to immobilize it and hold the pressure dressing in place. I decided not to give him morphine even though his wound must have been excruciatingly painful. I didn't want to have to carry him if we were overrun that night, which giving morphine might necessitate.

We had been resupplied with the indigenous rations of rice, shrimp, and peppers that would later become a staple. This was my first taste of those PIR rations, and they were the only thing I carried for food from then on. Perhaps they tasted so good because I was so hungry. Other advantages were that a single bag would last two or three days, they required less water to soften (one-third of a canteen vs. one-half for a LRRP ration), took up less space, and could be carried in my trouser cargo pocket for easy access. Whenever we stopped for a break, I would take a couple of mouthfuls and swallow them, then swallow a mouthful of water. When the water hit my stomach, the rice seemed to swell and it made me feel full.

That night I did not sleep one wink. Every 15 minutes I would check the Montagnard's dressing. He was amazingly quiet for the extent of his wound and must have had a very high threshold of pain. Having experienced the discomfort of simply hitting my crazy bone on occasion, I could not begin to comprehend the amount of pain in having the entire elbow shattered. After it got dark, the only way I could check on the dressing was by feel. Around two o'clock in the morning he began to moan slightly, and when I checked the dressing it was wet and warm. The backing I used to apply pressure to the wound was another combat dressing still wrapped in plastic, but the dressing tails had slipped off the unwrapped plastic covering. I tasted the wetness I was feeling to be sure it was blood and proceeded to apply a new pressure dressing. Since there was no way to provide light for what I was doing, I worked by touch and threw all sterile technique out the window. I literally had to feel for the smashed bones in his elbow to position the dressing properly. I guess I was successful at applying the new dressing as it did not become soaked and stayed relatively dry the rest of the night.

The Montagnard's discomfort increased and he began a periodic low moan, so I finally decided to give him morphine before he enabled the NVA to pinpoint our position. That quietened him down for the rest of the night, but I still did feel checks on his dressing every 15 minutes until it got light.

The next morning, we waited at the LZ until a helicopter picked up the wounded Montagnard, and we again moved out in a southwesterly direction. For the first time we split into two columns about 15 meters apart so we would only have to return fire to our left or right flank instead of having to cover both.

We sensed the enemy was near. I kept my eyes riveted on my field of view to my left, while intermittently scanning for cover to retreat to if shooting started. We stopped for a break and I took a couple of mouthfuls of the rice ration. Despite the heightened tension, I felt somewhat more secure knowing that I now had enough food and cigarettes to last another five days. There was no longer an urgency to being pulled out. I realized that I would be with the company for the remainder of the mission or until I came out on a stretcher or in a body bag.

It was mid-afternoon when we emerged from the jungle into a large area that was thick with brush and shrubs before becoming an open field of knee-high grass. Crossing the field, we came to a dirt road that was well used and well maintained. Once again, we were on a major branch of Highway 96. At the point where we intersected the road, there was a secondary road that also looked to be well used and headed southwest across a large open area toward a range of hills rising in the distance. There were a few 500-pound bomb craters, half-filled with water, just after the beginning of the secondary road. The area on either side of this road was clear for 30 to 50 meters up to the point where the jungle began. Our two columns veered farther apart, and we now walked along the edge of the wood line. I was placed well back in the column that was covering the area to the left of the road.

We had advanced approximately 150 meters when shooting broke out. We all hit the ground and began firing into the jungle nearest us. After firing three magazines or so, I stopped shooting and noticed I wasn't seeing or hearing anything that caused me to believe any fire was being returned. I looked around and saw Steve Roche three Montagnards to my right. I crouched down and moved over to his position and asked him if we were in contact.

He said, "I don't think so. I think we're having a mad minute." (A mad minute is an expression for when someone fires off a shot accidentally and everyone else starts shooting in the belief that they are in contact.)

"Let's go up front and see what is going on," he then said.

I followed Steve and we moved up the line of firing Montagnards to the head of our column. I was not prepared for what we were about to encounter.

The front of the column was mass confusion. The Montagnards were firing into the surrounding jungle, and there were explosions going off all around. I saw Bob Howard and Tom Jaeger on the ground beside an American, applying tourniquets to his legs. I approached and looked down at the wounded man's lower legs and saw that his foot was blown off cleanly at the ankle and attached to his leg only by the Achilles tendon. The other leg looked as if a giant hand had ripped out a chunk of his calf, exposing the tibia and fibula bones. I realized that there but for location lay me. The pearly whiteness of the exposed bone ends grabbed my attention. At the sight of this, I sensed a chill go up my spine and I felt myself getting weak like I was going to faint. This thought terrified me, and I said to myself, "You can't pass out. You might start a chain reaction and everyone will faint, and we'll all be killed." I tried to contract as many of my muscles I could. My body probably also gave me a shot of adrenaline at that time because the feeling of losing consciousness quickly faded.

I kneeled down to help Howard apply the tourniquets, but he was already finishing the second leg. I recognized the wounded American to be Lieutenant Swain, who had been on the mission since the Hatchet Platoon was inserted to reinforce Joe Walker and Team California. He was lying on his stomach with his chin resting on his crossed wrists and saying to Bob Howard that this would take care of his pheasant hunting.

I didn't know if he had seen the condition of his legs so I said, "Don't worry, sir, you're going to do a lot of pheasant hunting."

He replied, "What do you mean? My foot's blown off!"

I had no idea what to say to that and went back to working on the legs. Either Bob Howard or I administered a syrette of morphine because I remember pinning the empty tube to Lieutenant Swain's collar so the doctors after medevac would be aware morphine had been administered.

We were all told by Lieutenant Jaeger to keep our heads down because air strikes were about to be called in along the jungle edge in front of us. I saw branches being blown off the trees nearest us by the cluster bombs, and both Bob Howard and I received fragment wounds. I attempted to brush the fragment off my right calf because it felt like it was sitting on the skin and burning. It actually had penetrated into the muscle; the abundance of nerve endings in the skin only made it feel like it was sitting on the surface. Bob and I then resumed working on Lieutenant Swain's legs.

There was no problem in applying a dressing to the calf wound. The blown-off foot, however, presented a dilemma. I didn't want to cut the Achilles tendon, and his foot was still in his boot. The proper thing would have been to splint the leg, but with cluster bombs blowing the tops off trees within our perimeter, I felt it wasn't a good time to send someone into the woods to cut splints. I put a large combat dressing around Swain's severed ankle and repositioned his foot to as close to normal a position as possible. I then used another dressing to tie around the instep of the boot and extended the tails up to his calf, where I tied them rather tightly. Since he had tourniquets on both legs, I felt the tight tie would not add to any tissue damage. It looked good on the ground but would prove ineffective when we had to move him to the chopper later.

Just as I finished, two Montagnards approached me. One was helping another one along who was holding the right side of his face. When I had him move his hand, a half-inch flap of skin rolled down and hung off his jaw at nose level. It was like he had been scalped from eye to ear and then halfway down his jaw. I opened a combat dressing and eased the flap back up to its normal position.

At that moment I was interrupted by another Montagnard who said, "American wounded." He wanted me to follow him. I took the hand of the friend of the wounded Montagnard and showed him by putting my hand over his, how to hold the dressing in place and how much pressure to apply. I tried to communicate that I had to leave but would be back shortly.

I grabbed my M-16 and followed the Montagnard into the jungle, where we found the wounded American in a grove of small bamboo. He was kneeling on his haunches and saying, "I can't see, I can't see." I told him I was the medic and we were going to move him to the area with the other wounded. The bamboo grove was outside the defensive perimeter and thus subject to both our own air strikes and enemy attack. The Montagnard picked up the American's rifle and got hold of him under one armpit and I the other. We moved him, letting him face rearward while his legs dragged behind. As we approached the area where the wounded were, I could see what looked like machine gun bullets kicking up dust inside our perimeter, which on this side was more or less parallel with the wood line.

The American was an NCO, Sfc. Lee Dickerson, whom I had seen frequently in the club but never really met. His blindness was only temporary, but he had a fragment wound in his chest that I watched for maybe a minute. I was looking for the frothing blood that indicates a sucking chest wound, in which the chest cavity is no longer sealed and a collapsed lung can result. I didn't see anything to suggest that, but decided to treat it like one anyway. I removed the plastic from a combat dressing wrapper and laid the sterile side over the wound. I then taped it down with adhesive tape from my pack. I applied a dressing over that and tied the ends around his back. I didn't bother to try to apply pressure as the wound was not bleeding that badly and his pulse was strong. I was concerned with the possibility of internal bleeding, but there wasn't much I could do about it then except to monitor the strength of his pulse.

I returned to the Montagnard with the face wound and finished tying off the ends of the dressing and applying pressure. His friend had done an excellent job of holding the dressing in place, and the wound, as gruesome as it looked, did not bleed that badly.

By now I was really sucking wind, almost panting, and sweating profusely. I went back to Lieutenant Swain to check the tourniquets and make sure he hadn't started bleeding, when I got word there was another wounded. As I attempted to get up, I stumbled forward. I put my hands out in front to break my fall, but that didn't work and I nose-dived into the dirt. When I again tried to stand up, my legs were wobbly and I collapsed once more and rolled on my side. I had never felt so exhausted and nauseous. I told whoever was waiting for me I needed to rest. After a minute or two, I was able to continue but still felt weak and woozy.

There were several more wounded whom I helped bring into our perimeter. After an hour and a half since the first one, I gave Lieutenant Swain another shot of morphine, as he was beginning to show discomfort. I pinned the second empty syrette to his collar. The air strikes had been almost continuous since the start of the battle and we were trying to get a chopper in to extract the seriously wounded. My duties now consisted of continually moving from patient to patient, checking dressings, taking pulses, and trying to make the wounded as comfortable as possible. I began to be concerned about getting the wounded out before nightfall. I didn't want another night like the previous one with the wounded Montagnard. That would be the same thing but multiplied by 10 with the number of critically wounded we now had.

Yet again, Craig Collier of the 57th AHC Gladiators was providing slick support. On previous attempts to reach our perimeter, the helicopters were driven off by .51-caliber machine gun and small arms fire as well as three 37mm antiaircraft guns that were continually firing at any aircraft making a bombing run or that got too close. From the sound, it seemed to me that the guns were only two or three hundred meters to our northwest and we could definitely count three of them.

Running low on fuel the slicks would soon have to return to Dak To to refuel. Collier and his wingman, CW2 Carl Hoeck, came up with a plan to get in and get out with some of our critically wounded. First, Hoeck would pretend to fly off with the other slicks. Then, Collier would orbit at altitude and vector Hoeck back into the LZ at tree top level. Hoeck radioed the plan to the Covey Rider, S.Sgt. Mike Bingo, code name "Cheetah." It all seemed to work until Hoeck's ship came

CW2 Carl Hoeck, 57th AHC. His Huey, tail number 16-16167, was shot down attempting to medevac wounded after SLAM Company was ambushed on November 18, 1968. (Craig Collier photo)

to a hover approximately 100 feet above us and started to descend. A tracked vehicle with .51-caliber machine guns mounted on it opened up on Hoeck's Huey. Flames burst from the underside of the aircraft but Hoeck was able to auto rotate outside of our perimeter and crashed about 100 meters beyond.

My thoughts now were, "Oh no, I don't need any more wounded."

Bob Howard, Lieutenant Jaeger, and Lieutenant Price all ran out to lend assistance to the downed chopper crew. They returned a short time later with aircraft commander Hoeck, co-pilot 1st Lt. Fred Ledfors, crew chief Sp5c. Jerry Huffman, and the door gunner Sp4c. Bobby Gilmore, along with the chase medic S.Sgt. Tony Dorff.

A 37mm antiaircraft round had struck the ship on Gilmore's side, the impact slamming his head against the roof of the helicopter. Dorff, who inserted with the SLAM Company on the 14th and was wounded and medevac'd on the 16th, had volunteered to return to action as the medic on the extraction operation. When the slick hit the ground then bounced into the air he was thrown out. Both Dorff and Gilmore suffered injured backs as a result of the fiery crash.

As for crew chief Huffman, a .51-caliber tracer round that had come up through the bottom of the ship and hit the butt plate he was sitting on, continued smoldering beneath it. He was "kicking out the burning .51-caliber tracer round as if it mattered" as they auto-rotated before crashing. Upon impact, he was hurled against the transmission and temporarily stunned. Huffman recovered, however, and was instrumental

Sp4c. Bobby Gilmore – door gunner on Huey tail # 16-16167 shot down on November 18, 1968. (Jerry Huffman photo)

in getting Hoeck out of the helicopter as the aircraft commander's door had become jammed shut. The crew chief literally yanked the door open to free Hoeck. They then heard someone on the rescue detail calling "Over here, over here." They made their way as directed and followed Howard, Jaeger, and Price into the perimeter.

There wasn't much I could do for Dorff and Gilmore with their injured backs except get them sitting or lying down as comfortably as possible. A short time later, however, medic Dorff was up and helping me look after the wounded.

While I was busy administering first aid, I had laid my M-16 down somewhere within our perimeter. When I had a break, I went to retrieve it. As I picked it up, I noticed that it had taken a round through the stock, jamming the buffer spring. I checked the serial number and saw that this wasn't my rifle. Apparently, someone had swapped it for mine when his became disabled. So now I didn't even have a rifle that would

Sp5c. Jerry Huffman, crew chief of 57th AHC Huey tail number 16-16167 that was shot down on November 18, 1968. (Jerry Huffman photo)

shoot. I did have my .45-caliber pistol, but it wouldn't be of much use with only two clips of ammo.

More air strikes were called on the enemy positions where the 37mm guns were firing from. Word came to us that Sfc. Lloyd O'Daniel had silenced the .51-caliber machine guns on the tracked vehicle with a LAW (light anti-tank weapon) rocket. I recall an F-4 Phantom jet coming in so low you could make out the pilots. The jet dropped CBU, and you could see the canister split open and scatter a thunderstorm of explosions.

Approaching darkness was now my major concern. I knew it would be impossible to try to take care of all the wounded during the nighttime. Just before dusk, Lieutenant Collier made one more attempt to get in and successfully touched down. There were as many as eight people who really needed to be evacuated immediately.

I was helping to carry Lieutenant Swain to the helicopter and thought I had made it clear who should go out. When we got to the chopper, it was full of wounded so we had to pile Swain on the laps of some people already on the ship. Swain was screaming in pain as the chopper rose with his foot hanging over the side and dangling by the Achilles tendon. The chopper pulled out with 15 wounded plus the crew. Fortunately, most of the wounded were Montagnards, who didn't weigh as much as Americans. At least the most seriously wounded had been extracted.

A short time later another ship arrived, and we were able to get the downed chopper crew, Tony Dorff, and the rest of the critically wounded out. Before he was extracted, I swapped M-16s with Dorff so that I now had a working weapon. Hoeck and his co-pilot, Fred Ledfors, had been arguing about who would go out if only one of them could be extracted. Both wanted the other to go before himself. As it happened, there was room on the second medevac ship for the two of them so they were both ordered out. I was greatly relieved to have the critically wounded out before dark.

The Montagnards had been busy all this time, digging foxholes and forming an oval perimeter that could be defended since we would be spread exceedingly thin if we tried to defend the entire open area. I still had around 15 full magazines for my M-16, but was running critically low on combat dressings. I surrendered 10 magazines and three grenades for distribution to those who might be able to use them. Luckily, a number of the Americans carried extra combat dressings and partially replenished my supply.

I noticed one of the Montagnards' foxholes was not being claimed by anyone and went over to check it out. In the bottom of it was an unexploded CBU submunition. The American in the next foxhole invited me to join him in his, but when we both squatted down in it, we couldn't move around enough to shoot. For most of the evening we lay on our backs on the rear edge of the foxhole with our knees dangling down into it so we would have had only to slide in if we were attacked. After a while I moved back to the empty foxhole. I figured that if we were attacked, I would roll a grenade into it to explode the submunition then crawl in and use it as a fighting hole.

Initially, the assurance of air support all night long was not very comforting. When we were hit a few nights earlier, it had taken nearly two hours before the first bombs fell. This night would be different, but even after the jets had come in and dropped their payloads and expended their ordnance all around us, I experienced several anxious moments when they left and the sound of their engines faded. Each time, however, the uneasy silence would be broken by the distant drone of more approaching planes to continue the attack. At one point a "Spooky" C-47 gunship arrived, so we all got out our strobe lights and crouched down in the foxholes in order to outline our perimeter. I made sure I stayed away from the side of my foxhole with the unexploded CBU material.

The Spooky strike was very impressive. From the ground it appeared the red lines from the tracers were coming directly down at us, but at the last instant they seemed to bend and veer off. The shredding of the leaves from the mini-gun rounds ripping through the trees sounded like a summer hailstorm in a forest. The only difference was the loud cracking and thumping noise that followed—the result of the rounds impacting with the trees and ground. Around midnight one of the jets attacked the area where the 37mm guns were and struck an enemy ammo dump. There were secondary explosions for nearly three hours. For the first hour the small arms cook-offs sounded like a furious popcorn popper, interspersed with periodic loud booms and brilliant flashes that lit up the sky.

My feelings were mixed. I was glad the pilot had hit something big, but said to myself at the same time, "Boy, the NVA are going to be pissed now."

That night I tried to make my peace with God. I felt totally hypocritical in doing so, but recalled that God is all-forgiving and decided I had nothing to lose. I promised to try to be a better person if we were permitted to survive this night. This cemented my belief in a Creator, as I feel someone or something answered my prayers.

The air strikes continued unabated all through the night, and the sun rose on a fog-shrouded battlefield. It was my second straight night with no sleep. More air strikes were called around us, but there no longer seemed to be any return fire. After the sun had been up for about two hours, an NVA soldier came out of the jungle with his hands over his head. Bob Howard jumped up and ran out to accompany him into our perimeter. I think Bob was afraid the Montagnards would shoot him and had gone out to put himself in the line of fire so the 'Yards would hold theirs. I can't say those were his intentions, but that is how it looked to me as he escorted the prisoner.

Some of the Montagnards near us started motioning to cut the prisoner's throat, but we told them, "No! No! He beaucoup yap yap."

A short while later, two figures with weapons held above their heads approached from near where Roche and I had been when the battle started. This time the Montagnards didn't wait and opened up and fired for approximately a minute. After that the two men did not reappear, but no one felt like going out to see if they had been hit.

After the prisoner had been interrogated by the interpreter, I heard that he said we'd been ambushed by two companies of NVA. He further said there were a lot more of them in the woods around us who wanted to surrender, but they were all wounded. Also, he claimed that he did not carry a weapon, only supplies. About an hour later the extraction began and the choppers started to come in and take out six or seven persons each. When we were down to the last few chopper loads, one of the American officers told me to go out on the next one. I refused and said I would only leave on the last one because if anyone got hit after I left, I wasn't coming back down to treat them.

As the last extraction ship approached, we blew the claymores and got ready to board. I rode out with Bob Howard, Lieutenant Jaeger, and three other Americans. As we gained altitude, I felt like the entire world was being lifted from my shoulders. Tears started flowing from my eyes, and I couldn't stop them. I was sitting on the edge of the helicopter and stuck my face out into the stream of air. If Howard or any of the other Americans saw me, I wanted them to think the wind was just making my eyes water and I wasn't a candy ass.

◊ ◊ ◊

The events of the SLAM boosted my ego for maybe a month. Apart from the five indigenous personnel who were already dead when RT California and the Hatchet Platoon were pulled out on the 14th, no one else was lost on the mission despite the fact we had more than 45 wounded.

I must admit to having selfish motives as I treated the wounded. It was apparent during the battle that there was a distinct possibility that we would all be killed. I reasoned that my chances for survival rested in not only keeping the wounded alive but also keeping them in fighting shape.

The survival of the black NCO, Sp5c. Floyd Bryant, whom I had treated when we extracted the dead and wounded members of the Hatchet Platoon on the 14th, was directly due to the actions of Joe Walker. Had we not moved up to the platoon's RON position when we did, it is highly probable that he would not have lived. Likewise, the survival of Lieutenant Swain resulted from the immediate first aid administered by Bob Howard and Tom Jaeger. Had they not applied tourniquets immediately after he was wounded, it is likely Swain would have bled to death. I realized many were overlooking these facts when we discussed the events at the FOB after we had returned from the mission.

Bob Howard, Tom Jaeger, and I visited Sergeant Dickerson and Lieutenant Swain at the 71st Evacuation Hospital in Pleiku a couple of days after we were extracted. The prognosis for Dickerson was a complete recovery. The doctors had pinned Swain's foot back on and said it was probable that he might be able to walk on it if the reattachment was successful.

One thing I noted on this mission was the support by all the members of the company for the medic. Without the close cover fire that the Americans and Montagnards provided as I retrieved the wounded, I doubt that I could have been successful. I had the sense that most of the Americans would rather they take a round than the medic. I still owe a debt of gratitude to everyone who aided me in my efforts and kept me alive.

Having been on RT Ohio previously, several differences between SLAM and recon missions became apparent to me during the mission. Recon teams relied on stealth and silence, whereas SLAM companies were too large a body of people to remain as quiet as a recon team. When the company dug in, it seemed to me that it might as well have been shouting to the enemy, "We're over here!" as the entrenching tools clunked into the ground. It also dawned on me that the length of our column must have been a half a kilometer as we snaked through the jungle like a giant serpent. With roughly a five-meter spacing between men, a hundred-plus men equates to more than 500 meters. Whenever we stopped, for reasons unknown, it was frustrating trying to figure out what was going on. When you are a member of a long column, your world gets reduced to those immediately closest to you.

The one regret about the mission that I have is that I was so busy tending the wounded that I didn't see the many acts of extraordinary heroism that were going on around me. I was there, but missed one hell of a battle.

I would like to thank some other real heroes of SLAM VII. The pilots and crews of the 57th AHC Gladiator slicks, Cougar gunships, Kingbees, A1-E and A1-H Skyraiders, fast movers (jets), Covey, and the Spooky gunship can all take pride in the fact that they saved the lives of the entire company. There is no doubt in my mind we would all have been killed without air support. Their heroism, albeit unsung, is acknowledged and appreciated by me and by everyone who was on the ground in target area Juliett 9 during those five days in November 1968.

I would like to also thank the doctors and nurses at Dak To, the 71st Evacuation Hospital, and the rest of the locations our wounded were sent for treatment and rehabilitation. They tried for over a year to save Lieutenant Swain's foot, but eventually had to amputate it. He adapted well and worked as a crop duster after he was discharged from the Army.

You just can't keep a good man down.

It was following this mission that I began to have a different attitude toward the NVA—those soldiers whom we referred to as the "enemy." I realized they were just doing their job the same way we were. Like us, they were following the orders of those who were above them in rank and carrying out their duties as best they could. If the situation had ever presented itself, and a North Vietnamese soldier required medical attention, I would not have hesitated to treat him.

CHAPTER 17

After the SLAM—November Missions; The Loss of Ben Ide, December 19, 1968

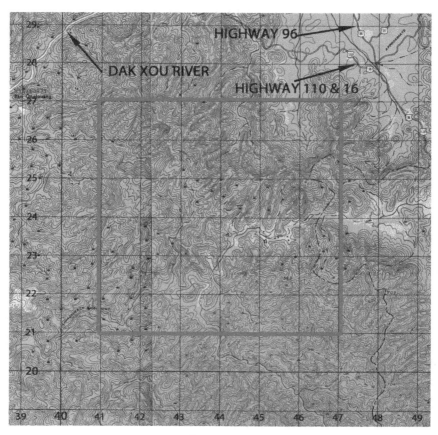

Target area November 9, 1968. (Joe Parnar map)

After the SLAM mission in Juliett 9, I returned to my chase medic and dispensary rotation. I learned that we had lost two recon team members while I was out with the SLAM Company. Sp4c. William M. Copley was MIA on a mission that had inserted on November 13 approximately 12 kilometers south of where our SLAM Company was ambushed. One-Zero S.Sgt. Roger Loe administered first aid to Copley under continued enemy pressure but was forced to leave when Copley's face turned white and the enemy threatened to overrun the team's position.

On 15 November, a Bright Light team consisting of several RT New Hampshire indigenous personnel, along with One-Zero 1st Lt. James D. Birchim and One-Two Sp4c. Frank L. Belletire, were sent in to try to recover Copley's body. After insertion, New Hampshire picked up enemy trackers almost immediately. Some of the team members ran off when enemy contact was made. Both Birchim and Belletire had been wounded when they reached an LZ where they could be extracted by McGuire rig.

CW2 Carl Hoeck, who was shot down medevac'ing our wounded on the 18th, was piloting the aircraft that picked up Birchim and Belletire. One of the four ropes dropped to the team got hung up in the trees so Birchim and Belletire tried rigging onto the same rope. Just after clearing the LZ, Hoeck flew into and was engulfed by a thunderstorm that struck the Laotian, tri-border, and Dak To area all the way to Kontum. Hoeck attempted to gain altitude and fly above the storm but had all he could do to keep the aircraft under control. By the time he finally made it through the storm, they were already past Dak To and low on fuel so he landed in Kontum. When they touched down, Belletire and the two indigenous personnel were covered in ice and Birchim was missing. Somewhere between Laos and Kontum he had fallen out of his rig.

November was turning out to be a bad month for FOB2, or CCC (Command and Control Central), as it had been re-designated by the MACV-SOG brass in Saigon. Neither Copley's nor Birchim's bodies would be recovered.

◊ ◊ ◊

I was working late in the dispensary on November 23 when S.Sgt. James R. Golding was brought in with a wound in the left side of his abdomen.

He and members of his team and two other Americans had gone to Kontum City where they got into a fight with some ARVN personnel, and a South Vietnamese officer shot him. Golding's blood pressure was exceedingly low, and we couldn't get a needle into a vein to start an IV. Judging from the location of the entry wound, it appeared the bullet had hit his spleen. A dust-off helicopter landed to take him to the 71st Evacuation Hospital in Pleiku, but he expired on the way. Several of the recon men wanted to go to Kontum to seek revenge on the ARVN, but the acting FOB Commander, Major Samuel Sanford, issued an order that no one was to leave the compound until further notice.

◊ ◊ ◊

On December 1, the 170th Assault Helicopter Company picked up the FOB2/CCC rotation from the 57th. I'm sure Craig Collier and Carl Hoeck were both glad to get a breather from our Prairie Fire and Daniel Boone missions. Things did not cool down in the target areas around the Bra for the 170th, however, and two helicopters were shot down on December 1.

One of the changes that had been made from when I was flying chase medic before my summer-time stint on recon with Texas and Ohio, was the helicopter gunship support. Each of the assault helicopter companies had their own "Charlie Model" gunships. These were basically Hueys outfitted with mini-guns and rocket pods. When I returned from recon in September 1968, the 170th AHC had begun deploying a single pair of Charlie model guns working in tandem while covering our missions, supplemented by a pair of Cobra gunships from the 361st Aviation Company (Escort), also known as the Pink Panthers. The Cobras flew 20 miles per hour faster than the Charlie models and had the advantage of a narrower profile when attacking targets straight on.

On December 1, one of the 170th's slicks was shot down along Highway 96 in Juliett 9. They were attempting to insert the second half of a recon team assigned a bomb damage assessment mission after a B-52 strike that was aimed at knocking out a hidden bridge on Highway 96. WO-1 Kent Harper, flying Bikini 29, successfully made it in and picked up the downed insertion chopper's passengers and crew.

One of the two Cobra gunships working the mission, flown by Captain Harold Goldman and WO Mark Clotfelter, took several .51-caliber hits and limped out of the area. They were able to set their Cobra down in tall elephant grass on a sandbar in the cleavage of the Bra. Despite this being one of the hottest areas of the FOB2/CCC area of operations, ringed with .51-caliber and 37mm antiaircraft guns, one of the other 170th slicks was able to successfully rescue the two-man Cobra crew. My chase slick did not go down to make the pickup but we watched the event unfold from 8,500 feet altitude. Goldman's wingman, Captain Gary Higgins then had the task of destroying the downed Cobra with his rockets.

◊ ◊ ◊

Approximately one week later, on December 8, 1968, One-Zero S.Sgt. Larry White, who had just returned to CCC, put together a makeshift team made up of One-Two Sp4c. Robert Clough, and straphanger Sfc. Bob Howard as acting One-One. There were five indigenous personnel accompanying the three Americans on the mission. The Zero-One (0-1), or indigenous team leader, was an ARVN sergeant and the remainder of the team were Montagnards. The mission was an area recon of target area November 9. There had been reports of unidentified helicopters being heard flying near this location and White's team was to investigate these reports. As with all cross-border missions, their secondary mission was to capture an enemy prisoner if the opportunity presented itself.

After aborting an attempted insertion on both the primary and secondary LZs, the helicopter attempted to descend into a third LZ just big enough for one chopper at a time to enter. As the aircraft touched down and One-Zero White jumped off, an estimated company of NVA opened fire on the helicopter and the disembarking team from all sides. The initial volley wounded Sergeant White but he was able to return fire into the enemy positions despite remaining completely exposed.

The initial blast of enemy fire also hit the door gunner and One-Two Clough, the second man out, knocking him back into the helicopter. Specialist Clough then dragged the wounded door gunner out of his

S.Sgt. Larry T. White—wounded on December 8, 1968 insertion. (John Plaster photo)

seat, laid him on the floor of the aircraft, and took over the gun. He placed extremely effective fire on the advancing enemy causing them to falter and retreat.

Meanwhile S.Sgt. White turned to assist some of his team members in re-boarding the helicopter and was wounded a second time by the advancing enemy. He turned and fired off a deadly burst of fire killing three NVA and wounding a fourth. As the Communist soldier fell, he shot Sergeant White again, wounding him in the chest. Although wounded a third time, White fired back and killed the falling enemy soldier. White then fell to the ground unconscious. His teammates pulled him on board where he regained consciousness and the chopper strained to lift out of the hot LZ.

As it was ascending to clear the trees and the crew and team returned fire, a round came up through the floor of the aircraft and hit the ARVN

Sgt. Robert E. (Buckwheat) Clough—wounded on December 8, 1968 insertion.
(Craig Davis photo)

Sfc. Robert L. Howard with shot-up Huey at Dak To airstrip, December 1968. (John Plaster photo)

team sergeant in the butt, killing him. The helicopter then flew directly to the 4th Division Medical Facility at Dak To.

The team members and crew reported seeing two helicopters parked under the trees on the edge of the LZ. These were identified as Russian Mi-4s. White also recalled seeing fuel drums and rubber fuel bladders near the parked helicopters.

White, Clough, and Howard were all awarded Purple Hearts for wounds received on the mission. One indigenous team member was KIA and the other four were wounded. The 170th AHC aircraft commander, co-pilot, crew chief, and door gunner were wounded as well. White was medevac'd to the 106th General Hospital at Kishine Barracks in Yokohama, Japan where he spent three months recuperating. In addition to their Purple Hearts, White was awarded a Bronze Star Medal for Valor and Clough and Howard were awarded Air Medals for Valor for their actions on the mission.

Because I was flying on one of the other helicopters and not on the insertion ship, there was nothing I could do to assist any of the wounded. After that mission, I always sat on a flak jacket if there was one available

Russian Mi-4 Helicopter. (Internet photo)

on the chase ship. The thought of getting shot up the butt from below gave me the creeps.

◊ ◊ ◊

When I reported to the helicopters to fly chase medic on December 19, 1968, the slick crew was buzzing about a hidden bridge that the Covey Pilot had spotted the day before on a tributary stream that entered the Dak Xou on the west side of the Bra. The bridge was located where the tributary stream crossed Highway 96 as it headed south.

The talk was that we were going to try to destroy the bridge with some homemade bombs that we would pick up at Dak To. This was to be a secondary mission following the insertion of a recon team.

At Dak To we met Bob Howard, who was preparing the bombs. He had started with four mini-gun ammo cans and put a layer of empty cartridge casings in the bottoms. He then stacked in quarter-pound blocks of TNT up the center, leaving room for more cartridge casings around the sides, and made two holes in the ammo can tops in what I thought was a unique manner. Lining up the lids on a small berm, he proceeded to shoot two holes in each with his .45-caliber pistol.

Next, he cut time fuses to the proper length. This had been determined on our trip to Dak To when a couple of officers riding on our slick threw out an ammo can with a sandbag in it from 2,000 feet and timed how long it took to hit the ground. Bob cut the fuses to the desired length, attached blasting caps, and eased them into the TNT. After placing a layer of cartridge casings on top, he threaded the fuses through the holes in the covers and clamped down the lids. Finally, he attached pull-type fuse lighters to each of the two fuses on the four bombs.

I was glad that the chase ship that I would be riding on had been chosen to be the slick bomber, as it would add a little excitement to the day. I believe the chase ship was selected because I could help pull the fuse lighters and push out the bombs. The slick pilots and crews were always a little jealous that the gunships had all the fun blowing things up and wanted a piece of the action. The aircraft commander of the chase ship that day was WO Kent Harper flying Bikini 29 who had picked up the crew and members of the recon team on December 1 when the insertion slick was shot down.

The insertion of the recon team went without incident, and we headed over to the area of the Bra for our bombing mission. When we got there, we went into an orbit at approximately 8,000 feet. The crew chief informed me that we would try our bombing run on the bridge after the Cobra gunships took a shot at it with their rockets.

A short time later he further informed me that the Cobras had seen a number of people in the open and were going down to "get them." Since no one was talking to a team on the ground, there was no commo

WO Kent Harper was flying Bikini 29 on December 19, 1968. (Russ Mowrey photo)

on my PRC-25 radio, and I was pretty much in the dark about what was happening

After a few minutes the crew chief and door gunner jumped up, and the three of us began pulling the fuse lighters and pushing out all four of the homemade bombs. I was confused because we had timed the bombs for 2,000 feet and were now pushing them out at 8,000. Also, we were not even close to the area where the bridge was supposed to be. I do remember that the resulting explosions were the loudest I heard while riding in a slick during my tour in Vietnam. That was probably because the bombs' airburst had taken place at around 5,000 to 6,000 feet.

We then began descending and wound up low-leveling about 10 feet above the water up the Dak Xou from south to north on the western side of the Bra. At one point we came to a split in the river and followed the right branch, which extended into Hotel 9, another one of our hottest target areas. After another 150 meters or so it came to a dead-end. The pilot reversed direction and flew back to the split in the river. He slowed and turned to the right, and we were now flying above the left branch. The chopper regained speed and continued up the Dak Xou. I was nearly in a panic trying to figure out what was going on. I thought maybe Harper and his crew were just "green" and thus unaware of the dangers in this area. My second thought was that maybe we were going down to get prisoners, a totally insane possibility. The last words I had heard rang in my brain— "… people in the open … going down to get them."

I was about to start shaking someone to tell the pilot to take it back up and stop screwing around, when we swung around to the left and I saw that one of the Cobras had nosed into the river bank. It looked to be 10 meters off the water's edge, right near the junction of the Dak Xou and the tributary where the underwater bridge was supposed to be located. The aircraft commander of the Cobra, Panther 12, 1st Lt. Paul Renner, was standing approximately 20 meters from the downed Cobra with his helmet under his arm and blood on his face. We landed close by, and I jumped out and asked him, "Where is the other guy?"

He responded, "He's in the ship. I can't get him out."

Knowing this was not an area we wanted to come back to, I said, "Let's go get him." Lieutenant Renner and I, along with a member of the slick crew, made our way through the brush toward the downed chopper.

As we were approaching the crash site, the other Cobra involved in the mission, Panther 16, piloted by aircraft commander Captain Gary Higgins and co-pilot Mark Clotfelter, made a gun run to cover us. I looked around and saw the mini-gun rounds hit the water on the tributary with the bridge. The best way I can think to describe what this looked like would be if one were to stand 15 feet back from a 10-foot puddle and throw a fistful of birdshot into it with one toss. It was as if 500 fish all jumped up out of the river at the same instant with a loud swoosh. It made me feel better seeing that, and I figured if I were the enemy, I certainly would not stick my head up and try to take a shot at us with that kind of fire coming in.

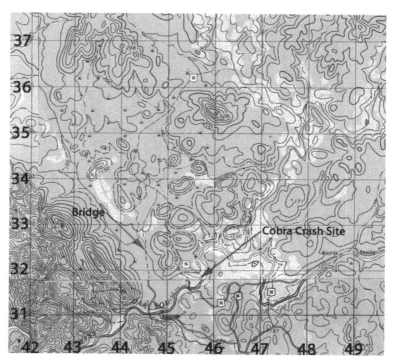

Ben Ide loss area. (Joe Parnar map)

We found the co-pilot/gunner, CWO Ben Ide, unconscious in the chopper. Lieutenant Renner ripped back the shattered canopy, and we lifted Ben out and carried him to the chase slick. I left my M-16 leaning against the side of the Cobra, as Ben Ide was a large man and it took both hands and all three of us to carry him. I never went back for the M-16 and hoped it was destroyed later on when the wreckage of the Cobra was bombed.

When we got onboard the slick, it immediately took off and either Lieutenant Renner or one of the slick crew cut off Ben's flak jacket and tossed it aside. His legs were badly mangled, so Renner and the crewmember began applying tourniquets to them. I felt for a pulse and found none. Ben was not breathing, so I began mouth-to-mouth resuscitation and external heart massage. This was the first real person I ever gave mouth-to-mouth to because we had always used dummies in training.

I tipped Ben's head back, pinched his nostrils, and blew in the first breath. Since I could see his chest rise as I blew air in, I lifted my mouth and began to take another breath. Immediately, I learned why when you

1st Lt. Paul Renner. (Paul Renner photo)

see people giving mouth-to-mouth, they turn their heads to the side after blowing in a breath. I had always thought it was to listen to hear the air coming out. But as Ben's first breath came out, a cold glob of phlegm shot from his mouth and into mine as I breathed in. It hit the back of my throat and gagged me almost to the point of vomiting. After the next breath I turned my head according to the book.

I estimated that it must have taken us at least five minutes to get to Ben after his ship went down, and I knew getting oxygen to his brain was of paramount importance. I continued my resuscitation efforts all the way to the 4th Division medical facility at Dak To, where the doctors relieved me with an air bag. I sensed I was going to lose Ben. I could not get his heart to start beating, and he had gotten progressively colder.

After he was taken off the chopper, the rest of us flew to our holding area off the main airstrip and shut down. We waited for word on Ben. An hour or so passed and then we learned that he was dead. I really felt terrible and began thinking of how I treated him. I immediately figured that since my actions were unsuccessful, my treatment was wrong. I chastised myself for not stopping the mouth-to-mouth and external heart massage when initial efforts were ineffective, and for not getting out my adrenaline needle and injecting it directly into his heart. I thought that if I had done that soon enough, I might have gotten his heart to start. I experienced so much guilt about this that to my mind it was almost as if I had killed Ben.

A short while later, the crew of the slick was looking at something so I approached the chopper. Someone had cut the canvas off Ben's breastplate, and you could see white impact marks where rounds had hit it. When they turned it over, it appeared as if the impacts had dented in the side that went against his chest. The consensus of the helicopter crew and pilots seemed to be that the rounds were probably .51 caliber. Again, guilt came over me because I had not even looked at the breastplate when it was cut off. In my mind this was another screw-up. I could only imagine that my chest compressions had probably driven broken ribs into Ben's heart, lungs, spleen, and liver.

My brain was a jumbled mass of confusion. It occurred to me that If Ben's ribs were actually shattered and I couldn't use chest compression to get his heart beating, then correct treatment, if there was any, was far beyond my medical capabilities. I didn't know what I could have done. I began to rationalize that if I had successfully resuscitated him maybe he would have been brain dead and a burden to his family for years. Before this, my philosophy of treatment had been to try to save everyone and keep them alive. It now hit me like a sledgehammer that being a real medic or real doctor demanded decisions that took into account that sometimes it might be in the best interest of the patient to discontinue resuscitation. It became clear that real medics and doctors must play God at times, and that was something I never wanted. I was coming up against too many questions that didn't have answers.

The next feeling that hit me was anger. I was angry that we had attempted to attack the bridge with our homemade bombs and gunship rockets. If the CCC commanding officers really wanted the bridge destroyed, why didn't they simply run a few more arc lights (B–52 strikes) through the area to take it out? All the screwing around had gotten Ben killed for nothing, in my opinion. I felt really down, so I turned to thinking about how I couldn't wait to get back to the base camp, where I would shower, eat, and get drunk in the club.

CWO Ben Ide. (Randie Ide photo)

Area of the Bra where Panther 12 was shot down on December 19, 1968. (Image © 2009 Digital Globe, Google Earth Point satellite photo, 2009)

Even though I continued the practice of trying to save everyone I could for the balance of my tour, the loss of Ben Ide made me decide that I didn't want anything to do with medicine or the medical profession once my tour in Vietnam was over.

CHAPTER 18

RT Florida, December 30, 1968–January 3, 1969—Christmas Eve Alert and a Prisoner Snatch Attempt in Cambodia

On Christmas Eve 1968, there was a show in the club. The featured entertainment was a live band that billed itself as Surfer Joe and the Surfaris. (The Surfaris were popular in the early 1960s and had the hit songs "Surfer Joe" and "Wipe Out." They broke up around 1966, but individual band members would periodically tour with their version of the band.)

Surfer Joe entertaining in the club on Christmas Eve 1968. (Joe Parnar photo)

Crowd at the club Christmas Eve show 1968. (Joe Parnar photo)

I sat with Ralph Rodd, Ken Worthley, Craig Davis, Dan Harvey, and Ron Brown during the performance. It was exceedingly hot in the packed club, and the band's drummer took off his shirt. I had brought my camera along and took several pictures. Meanwhile Brown, not much into surfer music, occupied himself by constructing a pyramid of empty beer cans on our table, a practice frowned upon by the CCC brass. After it accidentally got knocked over while the band was playing, some of the officers made Brown leave the club and that really pissed off the rest of us.

At one point someone started firing an automatic weapon somewhere along the wall. The "wall" was the outermost defensive barrier surrounding the compound and consisted of sandbag bunkers backed by stacked rows of barbed wire. The alert siren started wailing, and everyone in the club made a mad dash for their rooms to get their weapons and headed

Ralph Rodd manning RT Florida bunkers on the wall during Christmas Eve alert. (Joe Parnar photo)

RT Florida indigenous personnel manning the wall during alert. (Joe Parnar photo)

for the wall. By the time we had all taken our defensive positions, there was no more gunfire. It was decided that it was just a false alarm.

Whoever had pulled security duty that night probably figured that if they had to be on the wall, everyone else should be there, too. I took a picture of a couple of Rodd's team members on the wall and another one of Rodd standing on top of one of the bunkers in his black pajamas with his web gear and weapon. Rodd's Vietnamese team members thought it was rather funny that I was taking flash pictures during an alert. An

Christmas Eve alert casualty. Ran into barbed wire in the dark during alert and got some puncture wounds. (Joe Parnar photo)

Band members relaxing after the show on Christmas Eve. (Joe Parnar photo)

American had run into some barbed wire while running in the dark and was punctured across the stomach.

We all returned to the club and the band resumed playing and finished their show. I got to talk to a couple of the band members afterward, before the club closed. We said we were a reconnaissance unit but told them nothing concerning the details of the missions we were running. They asked us if alerts like the one we had that night were a common occurrence. I can't remember, but we probably lied and said they were. The show was the entertainment highlight of my stay at CCC.

◊ ◊ ◊

While I was rooming with Ralph Rodd and Ken Worthley, I tried to convince them that having a medic along on a prisoner snatch attempt could be a great asset. If the prisoner was wounded severely, a medic could keep his blood pressure up with an IV and otherwise treat him and keep him alive.

Over the course of several evenings, a group of us met in the club and we began planning just such a mission. I figured at this stage we were only pipe dreaming, as I had already been pulled off recon due to the shortage of medics in the dispensary, and that the powers that be would never let me go out. But I told Rodd he could make the offer that it could count as my R&R if I was permitted to accompany his team. We continued to fantasize about it with visions of a three-day trip to Taiwan and a $100 bonus for taking a prisoner dancing in our heads.

Our group included Sgt. Rodd, Sp4c. Worthley, Sgt. Dan Harvey, Sp4c. Craig Davis, and me. Harvey, Craig Davis, and I would be straphangers since we were not members of Team Florida. The likelihood of our dream becoming a reality seemed remote, as I couldn't recall a single recon operation into Cambodia that had more than three Americans.

You could have knocked me over with a pin when Rodd announced to us just before Christmas 1968 that he had gotten approval for the mission. Apparently, mission restrictions had changed, and more than three Americans were being allowed. Our planning now became dead serious.

Ralph R. Rodd, RT Florida One-Zero, December 1968. (Craig Davis photo)

Kenneth Worthley, RT Florida One-Two, December 1968. (Kent White photo)

Ralph would be the leader of the team that would consist of the five Americans as well as six indigenous personnel from RT Florida. Ken Worthley was going to carry the radio. I would carry a silenced Swedish K submachine gun for the prisoner snatch and a five-shot pump M–79 grenade launcher for firepower. Ralph reckoned that since I was so concerned with how bad we might wound the prisoner, I should be the one to shoot him. That seemed fair to me.

As the time approached for our launch, I drew the weapons I would carry from supply and prepared them for the mission. Cleaning the silencer for the Swedish K required scrubbing nearly 200 screen washers with a toothbrush and solvent to remove the carbon. After reassembling the weapon, I test-fired it to be sure it performed smoothly. I remember the loudest sound it emitted was the clacking of the bolt and a muffled *pfft, pfft*. I only fired about 10 rounds, as I didn't want to carbon up the screen baffles and increase the noise.

The pump M-79 I drew from supply had a malfunction and kept jamming whenever I attempted to fire it. After discussing the problem with Rodd, I swapped it for a regular M-79 grenade launcher.

Our plan was to set up an ambush along a trail and hopefully find an NVA or two whom we could take as prisoner. My part was to stand up and say *"Dung Lai!"* (Halt!) to the NVA, and shoot him in the legs with the silenced weapon. We would then secure our prisoner and make a run for the nearest LZ to be extracted. I would have a 1,000cc bottle of Ringer's lactate with me to boost his blood pressure if I wounded him too badly, and some morphine to sedate him if he resisted being captured.

The day before we were to be inserted, we had a mission briefing. This was the first one I had ever attended. Tommy Carr had always gone to them by himself when I was on RT Ohio. Also present at the briefing was Lt. Col. Roy Bahr, the commanding officer of CCC at that time. Rodd provided details of our objective—to take a prisoner; details of the area in Cambodia where we would be operating; and general information about the mission. Then each of the Americans on the team stood up and described his specific role and the equipment he would carry. I thought we did a good job at the briefing, and I got the feeling that Lieutenant Colonel Bahr was impressed at least by our enthusiasm.

On December 29, we all met in the club early in the evening. Actress Martha Raye was visiting and she came over to our table. She drank from a water glass full of gin while she talked to all of us. I asked her if she would be there awhile as I wanted to go back to my room and get my camera to get a picture with her. She said, "See me tomorrow. I'm going over to play poker with Major Jaks, and I'm going to clean his balls out." I didn't know if she was cleared for SOG missions and didn't want to say we would be in Cambodia the next day, so I never got my picture of Martha.

When she first came to the compound a few days before, I saw her ahead of me while I walked to chow one evening. Since Sergeant Major Arrowood was always prodding me to get a haircut and to shave off my mustache (probably because of my flunking promotion board), I wondered how the person walking ahead of me got away with such long hair. When she turned left to enter the mess hall, I realized it was

Martha Raye, an honorary lieutenant colonel in Special Forces. I guess sergeant majors didn't bug lieutenant colonels. By the time we returned from the field, she had departed from CCC.

Everyone retired early and the next morning was bright and sunny, so it looked like a sure bet the mission would be a go. I thought to myself as I returned from breakfast how for the first time in my life, I was exactly where I wanted to be. If the president had offered to send me anywhere in the world that morning, I would have requested to be with Rodd and RT Florida.

We inserted into Cambodia on December 30, 1968, using two Huey helicopters. Six team members were on one, and five were on the other. The LZ was covered with high elephant grass, and the indigenous interpreter sprained his ankle jumping off the first helicopter. What we originally thought would be a six-to-eight-foot jump turned out to be ten-to-twelve feet. The rotor wash from the chopper had bent the elephant grass over, concealing the fact that the ground was farther down than anticipated. The second chopper in had to snuggle deep down into the elephant grass so we could get the injured interpreter onboard at the same time the second half of the team was inserting.

Rodd moved us off the landing zone to begin the mission and radioed a "Team OK" to Covey. Later in the day we came upon a small bamboo shelter in the jungle with what looked like a sleeping platform built over the floor. The shelter was only about eight feet long and four feet wide, and we rested near it while taking notes on its construction. We could hear voices shouting in the valley a few hundred meters below us. While listening to these voices, I smiled at the indigenous personnel because I figured it meant the enemy was unaware of our presence and were being lax and careless. Since we no longer had an interpreter, we Americans had no idea what was being said. (After we got back from the mission, an interpreter debriefed the indigenous team members who reported that the NVA were saying something to the effect, "Come down and fight; we have guns." Sometimes ignorance is a blessing.)

Shortly before nightfall, we came upon a trail in the jungle. Our last team member had just crossed it and melted into the thick vegetation

Craig Davis, RT Wyoming One-Two, was strap-hanger with RT Florida on prisoner snatch attempt, December 30, 1968 to January 3, 1969. (Craig Davis photo)

when two NVA carrying weapons walked down the trail right behind us. They were no more than 10 meters away.

In order to conduct our prisoner snatch, we needed to have helicopters "on station," that is, ready to immediately come pick us up if and when we could secure a prisoner. With darkness about to fall within the hour, Rodd decided to RON a short distance from the trail and see if the two NVA would travel it the following morning.

To RON, we crawled and picked our way into the densest bamboo thicket we could find, cleared out a spot large enough to lie down in, and tried to get some sleep. The thickness of the vegetation gave us extra security, as the enemy would have had to make a lot of noise if they swept the area at night.

That evening there was an emergency going on not far from us. Bob Howard and a Hatchet Platoon had been inserted to try to recover the body of S.Sgt. Robert F. Scherdin, a recon team member who was MIA and presumed killed on December 29. The platoon commander, 1st Lt. James R. Jerson, had been seriously wounded during contact with the enemy. Ken Worthley listened through the night on his PRC–25 radio, monitoring these events and keeping us posted. We could hear the faint sounds of the battle in the distance.

The two NVA traveled the trail the following morning, December 31, but we were kept on hold as a good part of the day was spent extracting Howard and what remained of the Hatchet Platoon. We were advised to remain stationary and avoid enemy contact because no air assets would be available if we got into trouble. In addition, the normal inserting and extracting of teams for the day held priority over our prisoner snatch mission.

We spent New Year's Eve 1968 in the same RON location. During the night, other team members reported they could hear the enemy signaling by clacking bamboo sticks together. Apparently, I was asleep when this was happening. The following morning, the same two NVA made a pass down the trail just as they did the previous day. We were advised by radio contact that after the day's insertions and extractions, we could attempt our prisoner snatch.

Around mid-afternoon we moved to a position near the trail where we would attempt the snatch and waited for the helicopters to get on station. I applied fresh cammo to my face using my signal mirror to see what I was doing. After assembling the silenced Swedish K, I stowed the M–79 I had been carrying into my rucksack. I began to get extremely nervous as the time for the snatch approached. All of a sudden, the silenced weapon didn't seem to be more than a popgun, and I would have preferred some noise for its shock value. I felt that an NVA might see me stand up and start my clacking and *pffting*, then laugh and blow me away with his AK-47. I told Rodd to be sure his indigenous team members knew to shoot the enemy if he even looked like he was going to raise his weapon. Without the interpreter I don't know how I expected him to relay this to them, but just saying it helped ease my nerves.

We began hearing noises in the brush between ourselves and the trail. At first, I thought it might be some small animal rummaging in the leaf litter on the jungle floor. The noises kept getting closer and closer. After 15 minutes of strained listening, we heard a loud metallic click about five to ten meters from us that sounded like someone taking an AK-47 off safe. I turned my head back to look at Rodd, intending to make a motion with the Swedish K to see if he wanted me to fire at the sound. At that same time, one of the indigenous personnel had Rodd's attention and was indicating with two fingers that he could see people walking, and signified there were many by flashing all five fingers on his hand three or four times. Rodd motioned for us to move back from the area and we slowly withdrew from our planned ambush site.

After retreating approximately 50 meters, we began walking quite rapidly and hit another trail. We dogtrotted down this one and came to a junction of three other trails that were very well worn and recently used. Only one of them led away from the area we had just come from so we followed it. It took us to a river where we stopped to fill our canteens. I guarded the team with the silenced Swedish K pointed in the direction we were headed, ready to fire if anyone appeared. One of the Vietnamese came over and got two of my canteens and crawled through the brush to the water's edge to fill them.

We sought cover in what looked to be an old bomb crater that had filled in with silt when the river flooded, leaving a small circular berm about 20 feet in diameter. Rodd and Worthley called Covey to report we were on the run. We moved out and continued on the trail in the same direction. After traveling a short distance, we ended up back at the river. The point man began to wade across.

The far bank was the eroded and exposed side of a very steep hill, and the point man had to scramble up vines and brush to get to solid ground. A second indigenous team member had started to wade across, but after seeing the point man up to his chest in water, he elected to go another 20 meters upstream and utilize a huge tree that had fallen into the river. Its trunk was cracked in the middle, but the crown rested on the far bank. The remainder of the team took this route. It still required climbing up the steep banks through the brush and vines, but it kept everyone from becoming soaked. Running across the fallen tree, I felt like a duck in a shooting gallery. We wasted no time getting to the top of this hillside because we were open to view by anyone from the riverbank, which now lay below us.

We made our RON that night on the top of the hill where the ground leveled off. The next morning as we moved over the hilltop, we came upon a cemetery in the jungle. It was overgrown with vegetation but had headstones, some of which were quite elaborate. On top of one of the headstones was an NVA canteen and a couple of empty wine bottles. The canteen looked old and worn and was probably abandoned because it leaked. Craig Davis recalled having read that some cultures bury their dead with all their worldly possessions and thought to himself, "What a life." We did not touch the canteen for fear it might be booby-trapped.

The team slowly continued downhill toward the same river that had looped around the large hill we were now descending. About 100 meters from the river, we were forced to stop as we could hear numerous NVA along the bank, talking and chopping wood. We made our RON in this location for our fourth night.

The next morning, the start of our fifth day, I was out of water. When we had been at the river two days before, I had only given two empty canteens to the indigenous team member to fill. I figured it would take too long to dig the remaining two from my rucksack. I had an indigenous ration that I now softened with the Ringer's lactate I was carrying. I drank the rest since I felt our prisoner snatch attempt was now just a remote possibility at best. It tasted wet and relieved my thirst for the moment.

We began moving back up the hill the way we had come down because the NVA along the river were still there. Halfway up the hill we made contact with the enemy. Our point man and an indigenous team member named Chin heard a noise and crouched down behind some bushes while Rodd, about 10 meters behind them, also hid himself.

They saw three lead NVA soldiers and a dog they were using to track us. The NVA trackers released the dog, which came closer to Chin and the point man still crouching behind the bushes. The dog then stood on point like a bird dog. The enemy soldiers fired off a burst of rounds that kicked up the dirt in front of Rodd. Chin opened fire and shot all three NVA. There was a brief firefight with the rest of the trackers, and I got to shoot off two M-79 rounds before the team began immediate action to break contact. We headed down to the river toward a slightly different area from where we had heard the NVA earlier that morning. Rodd called for helicopters to extract us as we had enemy to our front and rear. The river was to our right and offered limited terrain in which to evade them.

Rodd stopped the team for a moment while he and Worthley talked to Covey. Craig Davis recalls that Chin took out a ballpoint pen and wrote the word "dog" on the palm of his hand and held it up to tell the other team members what had happened. Dan Harvey came up to me and told me that I had just stepped on a bamboo viper while we were coming down the hill. When I tried to speak, I found the salt water from the Ringer's lactate had puckered my mouth up like a prune and my tongue was stuck to the roof of my mouth. He asked me what was the matter and I mumbled, "I 'ank my 'inger's 'actate." Dan took out his canteen and offered me a drink. I was finally able to get my tongue and lips unstuck. Another lesson learned by experience.

Covey directed us to an area of 20-foot-high bamboo with an opening that did not permit a helicopter landing. We were informed we would have to be extracted by McGuire rig. Dan Harvey and I would go out on the first chopper with three of the indigenous team members. Rodd, Worthley, and Craig Davis would be extracted later with the remaining two Vietnamese.

The first extraction chopper came in and immediately began taking .30-caliber machine gun fire from the area of the river. The crew lowered a rope ladder made from aluminum and cable that was 60 feet long, so we did not have to rig Swiss seats for McGuire rig extraction.

The three indigenous personnel went up the ladder first, then me, with Dan Harvey bringing up the rear. The fire from the machine gun was getting very close, and the pilot pulled out while Dan was still several feet from the floor of the aircraft. The portion of the ladder below him was whipping toward the rear of the helicopter and I was concerned that it might get tangled up with the tail rotor. I was also afraid the flapping of the ladder would shake him off. I gave the team members in the ship

Sgt. Daniel R. Harvey—special projects and RT Florida in 1968 and 1969. (Dan Harvey photo)

a quick demonstration of how to hold my legs and lower me head-first down the ladder and helped secure Dan. I pulled him back so he could get both hands on the ladder rungs and a leg through one of the lower ones. I then motioned for the Vietnamese who were holding onto me to pull me back up into the chopper and got a Swiss seat sling rope and returned head first to tie Dan's arms to the ladder. I lurched forward when one of the Vietnamese holding my legs lost his grip and I screamed at him to not turn loose of my leg. I doubt he heard me over the noise of the engines and rotors.

The chopper pilots flew us to the radio relay site at Leghorn, a 20-minute ride, and hovered above the minefield. I untied Harvey and shouted into his ear not to go down the ladder to the ground as we were hovering over the minefield. He nodded he understood and followed me up the ladder into the Huey. We then headed for Dak To.

After we were all successfully extracted and the team was reunited on the airstrip at Dak To, I had one of the helicopter crewmembers take a picture of the team.

When we got back to the CCC compound at Kontum, Ralph and Dan Harvey called me into the team room and told me they were going to put me in for some kind of award for helping get Dan into the helicopter. I said I didn't want that and told Dan, "You would have been all right anyway."

"I don't know about that," he responded.

Ralph insisted on putting me in for an award and appeased me somewhat by telling me that it was a non-combat award. I dropped the issue, figuring it would just be some sort of "attaboy." I also had the greatest respect for Ralph and didn't want to argue with him.

The team photograph was far more important to me and is one of my most treasured souvenirs of Vietnam, especially so because Ken Worthley is in the picture.

Ken was KIA on August 26, 1969.

Worthley was one of the commo men with whom I had sat bitching and moaning in the club about not being on a recon team shortly after my arrival at FOB2. Each of them would eventually get his shot at recon, and for all but one, the results would be devastating.

RT Florida at Dak To airstrip on January 3, 1969 after prisoner snatch attempt. Back row (L-R): Unidentified, Ralph Rodd (without hat), Dan Harvey, Joe Parnar, and Ken Worthley. Bottom row, squatting right end, Craig Davis. Chieu (center) and three unidentified RT Florida team members. (Joe Parnar photo)

William Copley was MIA on November 16, 1968; Larry Stephens and Billy Simmons were KIA on January 29, 1969; Ron Bozikis was KIA on October 25, 1969. The only one to survive recon was Bob Garcia, who was on the mission when Worthley was KIA.

CHAPTER 19

Huey Crash—January 8, 1969

I was flying as chase medic when we picked up a recon team on January, 8, 1969, in Cambodia that had been inserted to search for the body of their teammate, S.Sgt. Robert F. Scherdin, who was lost on a mission on December, 29, 1968. The recon team was led by One–Zero Sfc. Gerald Apperson, and the One–Two was Sp4c. Bill F. Williams, Jr. They were accompanied by four of their indigenous personnel. This was the

S.Sgt. Gerald Apperson with indigenous team member. (Alan Apperson photo)

Sp4c. Bill F. Williams, Jr. (Williams family photo, supplied by Jason Hardy)

second unsuccessful attempt to locate Staff Sergeant Scherdin. The first was by the Hatchet Platoon, whose firefight with the enemy we had heard faintly in the distance during the night of December 30 while on the prisoner snatch operation in Cambodia. Sfc. Robert L. Howard had been recommended for the MOH on that operation and eventually received the award.

The first Huey from the 170th AHC to attempt the extraction, Bikini 119, piloted by aircraft commander WO Gary Odom and co-pilot 1st Lt. Jack Stanley, came under enemy fire and was damaged trying to maneuver into a very tight LZ. Crew chief Sp4c. Bill McDonald and door gunner Pfc. Joe Brooke reported the tail and main rotors were badly damaged and the ship was violently vibrating. Odom maneuvered his way out of the hole and headed directly back to Dak To.

The second ship in, Bikini 323, managed to pick up the team but also took enemy fire and we received word while heading back that they had taken hits and their transmission warning light was on. The aircraft commander, 1st Lt. Allen C. Gilles, opted to try to make it back to the Ben Het Special Forces Camp as it was the closest secure area to set down.

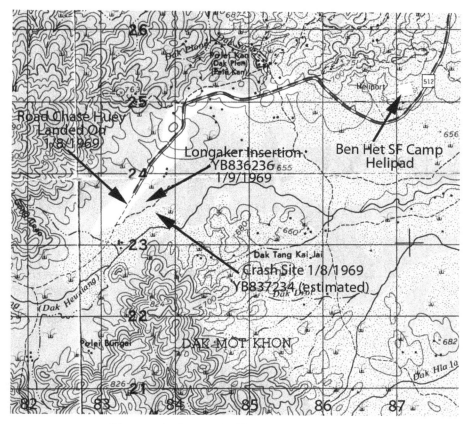

Huey crash, January 8, 1969. (Joe Parnar map)

From the chase ship we watched Bikini 323 for a while but it seemed to be flying with no problem and I went back to reading my paperback. As we approached the Special Forces camp at Ben Het, the crew seemed concerned with something off to the left side of our chopper. The door gunner got up to have a look, and I joined him. On the ground approximately four clicks southwest of the camp, smoke and flames were spewing out of the jungle vegetation. The extraction helicopter, piloted by Gilles, had crashed.

We began circling the area, then descended and landed on the road that headed southwest out of Ben Het toward the area of the old French fort. Another slick landed directly behind us. The pilot of the

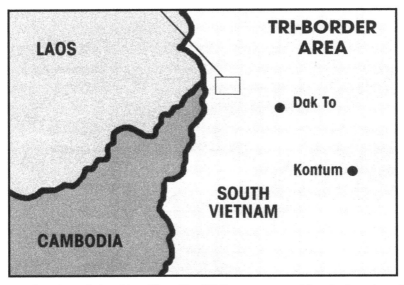

Inset map showing relationship of Ben Het SF Camp area to tri-border junction. (From original edition of *SOG Medic* by Paladin Press)

chase ship on which I was riding opened his door and climbed out of the Huey. At first, I thought there may have been something wrong with our helicopter and he was going to check it out, but he ran off into the single canopy jungle in the direction of the smoke and flames that were issuing from the downed chopper about a quarter-mile away. I was looking at the crew for instructions as to whether I should go with the pilot, when the co-pilot suddenly took off and began circling the area at relatively low altitude. The crew chief took the aircraft commander's empty seat.

A short time later the door gunner asked me if I knew how to rappel. I informed him I did and rigged a Swiss seat with my sling rope. I borrowed his gloves and connected into one of the four ropes used in McGuire rig extractions. The gloves were very thin, and I knew I would have to take it easy to avoid serious rope burns. My only previous rappelling experience was when I had trained with RT Ohio under Tommy Carr.

We had completed maybe three trips down the tower at FOB2/CCC, but they were all Hollywood rappels with no equipment.

I remember Tommy telling me that if you were carrying a particularly heavy load, you could run two loops around the snap-link instead of just one to slow your descent more. Since I now had my chase medic rucksack and web gear with grenades, water, and ammunition, I put two turns around the snap-link. The chase ship descended and came to a hover over an area where the height of the vegetation was lowest. I began my rappel. We were roughly 100 meters from the burning chopper, and I could clearly hear the exploding ordnance and small arms rounds cooking off. I immediately regretted the second loop on the snap-link as my progress was slow even without braking. Luckily, we were hovering only 20 feet or so above the treetops.

When I got to the treetops, I found them to be bamboo and about 35 feet high. The rotor wash from the chopper had bent them over, forming a twisted mesh of branches and stalks. I began wiggling, squirming, and kicking to work my way to the ground, which was still 15 to 20 feet below me. I was further hindered as I worked my way down by the fact that the lower portion of the rope was now above me and caught in the tangle of bamboo. When the door gunner threw out the sandbag and ropes, he threw out all 120 feet of rope even though we were only 55 to 60 feet off the ground. The extra rope was piled up on the tops of the bent over bamboo. I pulled the rope with my right hand so I could drop down a few feet at a time. I don't think the extra turn around the snap-link helped matters much. I finally reached the ground and opened the snap-link on my Swiss seat to disconnect from the rope rather than trying to pull the end through as it was still caught in the tops of the bamboo above me.

The crewman who loaned me his gloves then began to lower my PRC-25 radio with a rope as I had instructed him to do. I had enough sense to know that being on the ground with no commo was almost suicidal. Lowering the radio presented the same problems that I had experienced while fighting through the bamboo. It got hung up several times, but by following down the offending bamboo stalks and shaking them at ground level, I was able to get the radio to drop through. I thought to myself that this certainly was not a classic rappel and was glad I was not being graded on it. I untied the radio and waved for the helicopter to leave, and it departed the area.

I tried to contact Covey on my radio to find out what I should do, but no one responded to my call. I was on the same push (radio frequency) used when the team had been extracted, and perhaps Covey was now talking on another band with the pilots and not monitoring FM. I decided to make my way over to the downed ship. It was easy to find as the secondary explosions and small arms rounds and grenade cook-offs were intense. As I approached the area, I could hear rounds and fragments from the explosions shredding the leaves and vegetation above me. It was exceedingly noisy with the roar of the fiery helicopter, the crackling and popping of burning bamboo, and detonations from the grenades and small arms rounds.

I got as close as I dared and hunkered down behind a fallen log and decided to try to call Covey again. At that time someone tapped me

170th AHC crash site, January 8, 1969. KIA—170th AHC: Aircraft Commander Alan C. Gilles, Co-pilot Jon P. Roche, Crew Chief Robert D. Case, Door Gunner Steven D. Bartman; Special Forces: Sfc. Gerald F. Apperson, Sp4c. Bill F. Williams, Sfc. Bobby J. Dunham (Ben Het SF Camp). (Bryon Loucks photo)

on the left shoulder. I must have jumped a foot as I turned my head, half-expecting to see a muzzle flash from an enemy's AK-47. To my astonishment, it was an American I had never seen before. He told me not to go to the area to my right because there had been enemy fire from that direction, and he instructed me to follow him. I complied, and we skirted the crash site about 30 meters to the west where we met another American and some indigenous personnel. I saw the chase ship aircraft commander with this group and then the American who had led me advised me what was happening.

He said his name was Sfc. Bobby Dunham and that he was a member of a platoon that was part of a company-sized camp strike force on a search and clear operation out of Ben Het. Dunham and his second in command, S.Sgt. Richard V. Grier, were nearby when the chopper went down and had moved into the area to secure the crash site. He said they received enemy fire when first approaching the area, but there was no evidence of it at this time, only the explosions and the cook-offs.

We waited for a SOG Bright Light team to be inserted. I now had a better vantage point to see the downed ship and the fires that were still blazing all around the immediate vicinity. My concern quickly turned to whether there may have been any survivors who needed immediate attention. After coming through the bamboo maze a short time before, I felt it was possible that the trees could have broken the fall of someone falling out of the chopper before it hit the ground. I related this concern to Sergeant Dunham. After nearly a half hour, the cook-offs abated considerably, and we decided to go in and see if anyone was actually alive.

The ship was still a mass of flames. We approached to within 20 meters where we found the body of an American. I recognized it to be Sp4c. Bill F. Williams, one of the newer young recon enthusiasts at CCC. He was face down, and his fatigue pants were burning. I extinguished the flames as best I could and felt for a pulse. I found none and noted that the body had already cooled considerably. Dunham and I dragged Specialist Williams back to where the others were waiting. As we were dragging him, we noticed another body lying face down in some brush nearby. After we got Williams's body to relative safety away from the fires, we returned for the second body, which was that of an indigenous team member.

I got in position to lift the chest of the team member, and Sergeant Dunham took out his KA-BAR knife to cut back some brush sticking out from between the man's legs. He put down his knife and the instant we attempted to lift the body something exploded very close to us. The force of the explosion was like being hit in the right shoulder with a baseball bat at full swing. The blast propelled me nearly eight feet through the air. I can't be certain it didn't knock me out briefly because the next thing I remember was rolling onto my hands and knees and shouting, "I'm hit."

"So am I," answered Dunham.

I looked over and he was also rolling on the ground and coughing. I crawled over to him and observed a trickle of blood coming out of his mouth. I placed my arms under his shoulders, and began to drag him to where the others were. As I approached, the chase pilot and some of the platoon members came out and helped me carry him in.

I removed his shirt and began to examine him further. Sergeant Dunham had two small fragment wounds in his body. One was on the left chest slightly below and lateral to the left nipple. The other wound was a small fragment wound in the left temple area. His pulse was weak and thready, and he complained about not being able to breathe. I told him not to worry, and that I would breathe for him should he stop. He again said he could not breathe. I tried to start mouth-to-mouth on him but quickly found that unless the patient was unconscious, mouth-to-mouth could cause more discomfort than it alleviated.

A medevac for Sergeant Dunham was called. Since there was not a cut LZ on which to land, the extraction would be attempted by a Huey helicopter with a jungle penetrator—the first time I had seen one of the devices employed. I didn't think the medevac chopper was from SOG because it had a large red cross painted on it. It was probably a dust-off ship from the 4th Division at Dak To since the crash had occurred well within Vietnamese territory. We got Dunham to the LZ and decided that we would have to tie him to the penetrator since he was barely conscious. This turned out to be unnecessary when the slick pilot who had run into the woods earlier volunteered to straddle the penetrator's legs and hold Sergeant Dunham in his arms for the ride up by winch to the chopper. Without his quick thinking, it would have taken a lot longer to medevac the wounded NCO.

A short time later the SOG Bright Light team rappelled into the area where we had winched out Sergeant Dunham. It was RT Maine led by One-Zero S.Sgt. Daniel W. Janc. The team began cutting an LZ where they had rappelled in, and I waited around for another medic to replace me. I had taken a fragment in the right shoulder as a result of the explosion and wasn't going to be of much use any longer. I did make sure no one approached the downed ship until the cook-offs had stopped to avoid losing anyone else.

After the LZ was cleared, the SOG chase ship approached with Sgt. Bryon Loucks, the replacement medic. I gave him a sit-rep on the crash and got on the helicopter and was flown to the medical facility at Dak To.

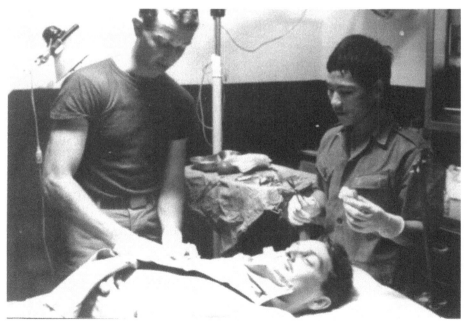

Sfc. Louis Maggio sutures a wound on Joe Parnar in the CCC operating room on January 8, 1969. Parnar was injured by an explosion during a mission to try to recover the body of S.Sgt. Robert Scherdin. (Bryon Loucks photo)

The medical personnel there told me that Sergeant Dunham was still alive when he arrived at Dak To and had been immediately sent to the 71st Evacuation Hospital at Pleiku for surgery. They probed my shoulder and dressed it. I then returned to the helicopter holding area off the main airstrip. I gave back the gloves, slightly rope-scarred, to the Huey crewmember and flew back to Kontum with the slicks at the end of the day.

When I got back to Kontum the head medic, Sfc. Lou Maggio, examined and probed the wound again and determined it would be better to leave the fragment in rather than try to remove it and cause further tissue trauma. He placed my right arm in a sling and put me on light duty for a week. That meant no flying chase medic. That night I noticed how much I relied on my right hand when I had to drink my beer with my left. It felt alien and awkward.

The following day I learned that Dunham had died. The word I got was that he underwent open-heart surgery and did not respond, so they took him into brain surgery and he never came out of the anesthesia. I once again experienced enormous guilt feelings, as I felt my actions in pushing to search for bodies before the area was safe was instrumental in Sergeant Dunham's death. My guilt was compounded when it became known that no one had survived the crash. I felt I had contributed to the death of a person trying to rescue dead bodies.

On January 9 a Hatchet Platoon led by 1st Lt. Frank Longaker went in to police up weapons and remains from the crash site. With him were Sergeant Tandy and Sergeant Jones. Bryon Loucks also accompanied the platoon. They were inserted about 200 meters northwest of the crash site and located it without difficulty. They removed several bodies that were trapped in the ship when it had gone down and destroyed any damaged weapons and unexploded ordnance remaining in the immediate area with C-4 explosives.

Lost were Sfc. Gerald Apperson and Sp4c. Bill F. Williams, along with four of their 'Yards from the recon company at CCC, and Sfc. Bobby J. Dunham, assigned to the isolated Special Forces camp at Ben Het (Camp A-244). Also killed were the slick pilots and crew. These included aircraft commander 1st Lt. Alan C. Gilles, co-pilot WO John P. Roche, crew

Co-pilot WO Jon P. Roche. (William Roche photo)

chief Sp4c. Robert D. Case, and door gunner Sp4c. Steven D. Bartman. (The names of the crew were originally supplied to me by Jim Williams, Panther 033, a Cobra gunship pilot who provided gunship support for our missions.) Sfc. Dunham was posthumously awarded a Silver Star for Valor for his efforts in the rescue attempt, and S.Sgt. Grier received a Bronze Star with V device.

The attempts to rescue/recover Sergeant Scherdin came at a high price. Eight Americans made the ultimate sacrifice, as did a number of indigenous personnel during the Hatchet Platoon's and recon team's recovery efforts. Scherdin's body was never found.

CHAPTER 20

Wiretap Recovery with a Hatchet Platoon—February 1969

January also proved to be a bad month for CCC. On the 29th, every American on Recon Team New Mexico was KIA on a mission in Laos. They were S.Sgt. Charles D. Bullard, Sgt. Billy J. Simmons, and Sp5c. Larry A. Stephens.

On January 30, Sp4c. Jerald J. Bulin was KIA on the nightly security patrol around the base camp at Kontum. There were NVA troops in the area at the time, and the 'Yard camp had been hit one night. Bulin had arrived at CCC only a couple of days before. That brought the total Americans lost in January to six, the highest loss count for any month of my tour. And this did not include the four crewmembers of the Huey from the 170th AHC lost on January 8 supporting CCC recon operations.

In February one of the recon teams located an enemy telephone line along a road network of the Ho Chi Minh Trail that skirted the Vietnamese border just inside northern Cambodia. They decided to plant a wiretap, a suitcase-sized device designed to record the messages sent over the tapped line and relay them to a plane that would periodically fly overhead. After planting the wiretap, the team withdrew a few hundred meters to RON for the night.

During the night, the team had an emergency when the enemy seemed to be cutting a road right up to their position. A firefight ensued, and they were extracted the following morning. About a week later a Hatchet

Platoon of approximately 35 men was to be inserted to recover the device because it had stopped transmitting messages. One of the Americans from the team that had planted the wiretap accompanied the platoon to assist in locating it. I was the medic assigned to accompany the platoon.

The mission was launched from the CCC compound at Kontum instead of the normal launch site at Dak To. This was because the flight to Dak To would have been longer than the distance to our target area. We were dropped off in Vietnam roughly a mile from the Cambodian border.

The insertion was accomplished without incident, and we proceeded west toward Cambodia. We traveled up and over two small, moderately steep hills and then hit an enemy trail with bunkers built on either side every 10 to 20 meters. We also could hear people talking in the jungle off the side of the trail to our north. They may have been cutting wood because we could hear periodic chopping. We crept up this trail and past those doing the talking, who I would estimate were maybe 30 meters away. The trail seemed to follow a ridgeline, and as we got to where the ground leveled off, we stopped when we heard sounds we couldn't identify. It was as if someone was shouting something followed by a multiple cracking noise. All I could picture was someone practicing karate chops on a shattered piece of bamboo.

The commander of the Hatchet Force, a first lieutenant, sent a small detail to see what was causing the sound. When they returned, they advised that there was a large number of NVA out in the open doing drills with their rifles. The shouts we were hearing were those of the drill sergeant calling out the orders, and the cracking noise was the soldiers slapping their weapons while executing the commands. It raised the hair on the back of my neck to know the enemy was so very close by. At this point, I noticed we had stopped just before a three-feet-in-diameter tree trunk that had fallen across the trail, and the detail that was sent forward had to climb over it.

After calling for a Covey plane, the first lieutenant proposed going back down the trail the way we had come up. When the word was relayed to the rear of the column, an American came to the front and said that one of the Montagnards had overheard one of the NVA who was cutting wood say, "We will get them when they come down." After confirming this with the indigenous interpreter and the Montagnard, the first lieutenant then directed the column to angle off the ridgeline at approximately 45 degrees in a southeasterly direction. I was glad the lieutenant listened to reason and decided not to go back down the trail.

I was positioned near the middle of our single column and was about 40 meters below the ridgeline trail when a Bird Dog spotter plane from the 219th Aviation Company out of Pleiku, the Headhunters, flew across the trail above us. A half-dozen AK-47s immediately opened up on it. Our commander, hearing the shooting and believing we were under fire, tossed a purple smoke grenade.

The purple smoke drifted up the hill toward the NVA who had been doing the shooting. They must have thought the pilot had thrown out the smoke grenade when they fired on the plane, as there were no rounds now being directed down at us.

We continued downhill another 50 meters and crossed a small brook and started up another hill whose ridgeline intersected with that of the hill where we had seen the NVA 100 meters or so to our west. We walked another 75 meters up this hillside, then sought cover and made preparations to call in an artillery strike.

We were now almost exactly on the border of Vietnam and Cambodia. The plan was to walk the artillery up the ridgeline and trail we had traveled earlier into the concentration of the enemy. We received word from our radio operator that the Bird Dog pilot reported that in his multiple tours in Vietnam, he had never seen so many NVA out in the open.

The artillery took a while to get under way, but eventually three-round salvos began progressing up the ridgeline and into the enemy's position. All at once the NVA seemed to panic and started intermittently firing at the Bird Dog with 37mm antiaircraft guns, a .51-caliber machine gun, and countless numbers of AK-47s. Judging from the din resulting from the simultaneous discharge of the antiaircraft guns, it sounded as if there were three of them.

After the artillery had reached the top of the hill where the two ridgelines joined, it continued for almost another hour, still in three-round salvos. All the while the enemy guns fired at the spotter plane, as if the NVA felt this was the source of their problems.

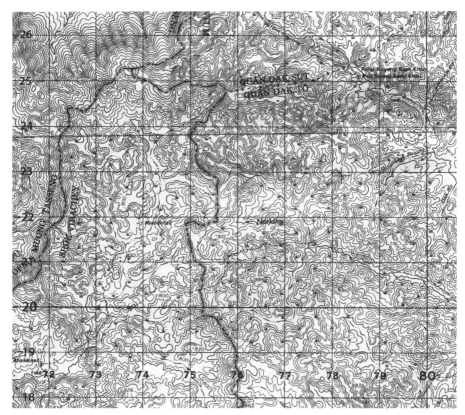

Somewhere near the Cambodian border in the first six or seven kilometers south of the tri-border junction, the wiretap recovery mission occurred. Exact location is uncertain. (Joe Parnar map)

After the artillery had finished expending, we were told to still keep our heads down. We would be getting air support from some Navy jets that had taken off from an aircraft carrier and they would be dropping 500-pound bombs. We sought cover behind what trees and logs we could find as the air strikes began.

The show was awesome. We could tell whenever one of the jets was approaching as the three 37mm antiaircraft guns would open up, along with the .51-caliber machine gun and all the AKs up on the hilltop. The firing would stop abruptly and after a short pause there would come the noise of the exploding bomb. Six-inch pieces of smoking bomb casing fragments were dropping through the trees around us. After the explosion, the next thing we heard was the roar of the jet passing and then the sounds of the flak from the 37mm rounds popping off high in the air. We stayed in our positions and listened to the air attack all afternoon until it got dark. We were advised that this would be our RON location for the night.

The night passed without incident and the next morning the air strikes continued, but now there was no return enemy fire. Around midday we proceeded south to recover the wiretap. We went up and over two more ridgelines of hills about the same size as the one where we had encountered the NVA. At a third one we found evidence of a road having been cut and the member of the recon team that had planted the wiretap identified this as the area of their RON. He then located the place where the team had tapped the wire, but both the wire and wiretap device were gone.

We followed the unfinished road to its source and found it connected to a well-used and well-maintained dirt road that skirted the border just inside Cambodia. We continued walking north alongside this road roughly 20 meters off to the Vietnam side and in the jungle. The Hatchet Platoon commander was then told to return to the area where the air strikes had taken place and do a bomb and artillery damage assessment.

After paralleling the road for another half-mile, we found a side road that headed east toward Vietnam. You could tell it was new because there were still small stumps and vegetation on the roadbed. We followed it until it opened up onto the hilltop where the two ridgelines joined, the site that had been the target of our artillery and air strikes the previous day.

We discovered an enemy complex that was quite well laid out. There were even urinals and latrines built into the ground. We could tell that the three 37mmm antiaircraft guns had been positioned in the form of a triangle, with six-foot-deep trenches connecting them like three spokes in a wheel coming together in the center. There were cave-like bunkers dug into the walls of the trenches every 10 to 15 feet. The guns themselves had been set into large foxholes approximately 15 feet in diameter. Where one of the gun positions had been there now was a 500-pound bomb crater that half-overlapped the original hole. We found the recoil spring from the gun in the pit. There were numerous empty 37mm casings around the gun pits, and I put one in my pack as a souvenir. Someone else found an unfired shell and took it with him.

Near the latrines, I found clumps of human hair. Either an NVA barbershop was once there or someone had been seriously wounded. There also were numerous bloodstains on the ground. We found no bodies in the area because the NVA took everything when they abandoned the position the previous night. It was my theory that after laying their wiretap, the recon team was surprised by the same NVA forces that we had called artillery strikes on and the Navy jets had bombed. I guessed they were building the road to move the antiaircraft guns into place when the recon team made contact with them. They redeployed three ridgelines north, feeling the initial site was too hot after their firefight with the recon team. We had subsequently encountered them in their new position.

As we were leaving the area, we came across the huge tree that I had noticed the day before when we stopped to investigate the strange sounds. It was only about 20 meters from the enemy latrines. It looked to me like the enemy had cut it down to clear the field of fire for their gun position. We then traveled down the trail we had come up the day before and veered off when Covey directed us to an LZ. We were extracted without incident late in the second day, just before dark.

In my estimation this was probably the most successful mission in which I participated despite the fact we did not recover the wiretap device. We got extremely close to the NVA, called in artillery and air strikes on them for most of a day, knocking out one of their 37mm guns, and made them abandon their position—all without having a shot directly fired at us.

CHAPTER 21

SLAM Replacement Mission—March 1969

I was flying chase medic on a day a SLAM Company was going to be extracted and replaced with a fresh company. The operation had started with a recon team being extracted from a bomb crater LZ. Because the recon team reported signs of enemy activity, a SLAM Company was inserted a day or two later. The company conducted a reconnaissance by force mission in an area of southern Laos near the border with Cambodia and Vietnam. They had been in for about five days and had one Montagnard KIA and had been carrying his body for more than a day. The fresh company would replace them to continue the sweep.

Since the company consisted of more than a hundred men, it was going to take eight helicopters to complete the insertion and extraction. Four of the ships were Huey slicks and four were Kingbees. Two separate flights from Dak To by the eight ships would be necessary in order to make the exchange. The Kingbees would insert the SLAM commander and lead elements, and the Hueys would insert the balance of the first half of the company.

Because the company on the ground was on the move and carrying their KIA, it had not reached or secured a landing zone. The plan was to insert the fresh company and allow them to secure the LZ. The company already on the ground would then be extracted once they had reached and linked up with the replacement company.

The Covey Rider that day was Sp5c. James M. "Mike" Tramel, code name "Menace". The LZ for the insertion was a large opening approximately 50 meters wide, with several trees interspersed across it.

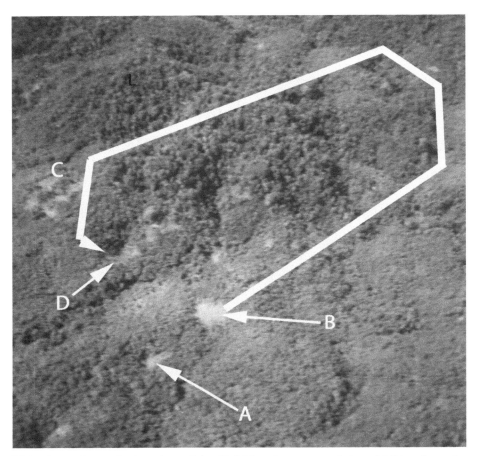

This photo shows the location of the SLAM replacement mission. "A" is where the recon team was extracted identifying the area as a "hot" target. "B" is where the original SLAM Company was inserted. The looping path that ends at point "C" indicates the approximate route of the five-day sweep. "C" is where the company got into a fire fight and called in multiple air strikes, and "D" is the LZ where the swap of companies was accomplished. (Joe Parnar photo)

A large bomb had probably been used to create the LZ at one time or another, and it was littered with debris.

The Kingbee lead made its approach, but the pilot found he could not get down on the ground because of the trees. None of the Kingbees were rigged to allow the company to rappel in. The pilots of the Huey slicks, however, felt they could get into the LZ.

Leghorn Radio Relay site, Laos. Located about 10.4 miles northwest of the tri-border junction, it enabled communications with the recon teams operating in southern Laos and northern Cambodia. (Joe Parnar photo)

Mike came up with the following contingency plan: he would have the Kingbees head for the radio relay site at Leghorn and drop off their element while the Hueys inserted their personnel. The Hueys would then follow the Kingbees back to Leghorn to pick up the lead element and return to the LZ and insert them. The reason he selected Leghorn for the drop-off and pickup point was because it was considerably closer to the LZ than Ben Het or Dak To or any other secure site in Vietnam. The flight to Leghorn was only 20 minutes compared to 30 minutes or better to Ben Het and Dak To.

Shortly after the insertion of the second half of the element by the Hueys, a serious problem arose. When Mike attempted to make contact with them, he realized that the radio was on a Kingbee with the lead element of the company on its way to Leghorn. The personnel on the ground had no commo. Any unit operating in this area of Laos would be in grave peril without the ability to communicate with the aircraft overhead.

Part of the equipment carried by the chase medic was a spare PRC-25 radio. This was used at times to communicate with Covey when the choppers would shut down at Dak To awaiting launch orders. (When the choppers were shut down, so were their radios.) The PRC-25 was also used as an emergency backup if a team on the ground had a bad radio.

The crew chief of the chase slick I was riding on told me that we were going down to drop off the spare radio to the element on the ground.

As we came to a hover about 10 feet over the LZ, I could see a line of Montagnards moving up the hillside to secure the high ground. The last one in line looked at me, and I waved for him to come back and pointed to the radio. I did this a couple times but he then turned and continued up the hill. I didn't know what to do next, but it was imperative that I deliver the radio.

I jumped off the helicopter with the radio in one hand and concentrated on not slamming it into the ground. I was wearing my web gear and had my chase medic pack on my back. My M-16 was slung over my head and shoulders. When I jumped, the chopper was still hovering at 10 feet, and when I hit, I fell forward and stuck my rifle muzzle into the ground. The sight prevented it from going deeper than six inches and I had put adhesive tape over the muzzle, so it didn't get dirt in the barrel. I quickly got up and waved for the helicopter to leave and proceeded up the hill after the last Montagnard.

When I caught up to him, I said, "American? Where American?"

He looked at me puzzled and smiled. He probably was thinking to himself, "No shit, I can see you are an American, stupid."

I then went up to the next Montagnard and attempted the same questioning and got the same result. None of them could speak English, and I spoke no Montagnard. After trying this on three or four more of them, I gave up and decided to call Covey and advise him of the situation.

My code name with SOG was "Transistor," so I turned on the radio, pressed the send button down on the hand piece to transmit, and said, "Covey, Covey, this is Transistor, Transistor—Over."

Tramel responded, "Transistor, this is Covey. What the hell are you doing down there?"

I told him there was no one on the LZ to accept the fox mike (PRC-25 radio) so I had to get off. I also advised him that I appeared to be the only straw hat (code word for American) on the ground. I was still talking to Mike when another American came down the hill and I said I would turn the radio over to him. Apparently, the fellow was not familiar with the PRC-25 and seemed confused when talking to Covey. He finally said, "I don't know what to say, you do it," and handed the radio and hand piece back to me.

I got back on the radio with Tramel and he told me we needed to blow some of the trees off the LZ because even the Huey slicks were having trouble touching down. That was the reason for my 10-foot jump. I asked the other American if he knew how to use demolitions. He replied he did, and I pointed out the trees to blow and reported back to Covey.

Tramel advised me the company being relieved was approximately a quarter-mile away and slowly working their way to our position. He said to fire a shot in the air so they could pinpoint our location. We did this several times during the linkup. I told the American to better disperse the Montagnards around the upper border of the LZ so we would have control of all the high ground and fields of fire for the entire open area.

About 45 minutes later the Hueys returned with the commander and lead element. The three small trees that had caused most of the problems initially had been cleared by the American, and the helicopters now had no trouble setting down. I talked to Tramel, and he ordered me to get my ass on the first one out after it unloaded. Just as the lead Huey landed, the company being relieved entered our perimeter. I boarded the empty chopper with my radio, leaving the other American on the ground to brief the commander.

I didn't know if I was going to be in trouble or not for abandoning my chase medic post, but I believed in my mind I had done the right thing. I thought of Pappy Webb and the lesson he taught me concerning teamwork when I was on ST Texas. I felt Pappy would have been pleased knowing his message had sunk in.

We had accomplished the changeover and safely extracted the SLAM Company that needed relief. After a long day we returned to the CCC base at Kontum.

That evening Mike Tramel came to my room to see me. At first, I thought I was going to get chewed out, but he told me I had really saved the mission and prevented what could have been a disaster. He said he wanted to put me in for an Air Medal and asked me how it felt to be a SLAM commander. I laughed at the SLAM commander bit, but did feel complimented. I asked him not to bother with the award, explaining I was only doing my job and did what any of the other chase medics would have done. I also explained that I would be out of the Army in another month or so and told him to save the award for someone who was a career soldier and would have some use for or benefit from it.

CHAPTER 22

Final Missions, March 1969—Attack on CCC Headquarters at Kontum, Extraction of James Ripanti, and Medevac of Burned Montagnards

On March 2, 1969, enemy RPG rockets hit CCC headquarters, with three or four actually penetrating our defensive perimeter.

By then I had been in Vietnam 11 months, and at FOB2/CCC for nine and a half months. My roommate at the time of the rocket attack was Bryon Loucks, a fellow medic and classmate from Medic training at Fort Bragg. A third roommate was about to join us—Sgt. John Walton, who was in the same medical class with Bryon and me. He had dropped off his gear that afternoon and gone to the club where he got into an all-night poker game. John was at FOB1 at Phu Bai originally, but came to CCC early in 1969 when Phu Bai closed down. He had been assigned to the 'Yard camp down the road and was coming to the CCC compound for his final month before DEROS. I thought it was quite a coincidence that three medics who all graduated in the same class would be roommates for their last month in Vietnam. I thought this might be a record of some kind, if anyone kept track of such things.

But the record was not to be.

I had gotten in late as usual after the club had closed. Around 0400 hours, we were awakened by a loud bang. At first, I thought it might be someone firing the 4.2 mortar from the pit near our room, but realized it was incoming when I could hear sand tinkling down on the metal roof of the building.

I called to Bryon, "It's incoming! Get under your bunk!"

The idea of diving under our bunks had flashed into my head as a result of having seen signs with exactly those instructions on the walls

Rocket attack on CCC Headquarters on March 2, 1969. B-40 RPG wounded Bryon Loucks and Joe Parnar. (Paul Morris aerial photo)

of the 71st Evacuation Hospital at Pleiku where I had visited some of our wounded. I got under my bunk and looked back toward the door and remembered I had not latched it when I came in before because Walton was still at his poker game. I could see it was slightly ajar. Then the warning siren began to wail, which meant we were being hit. Because of the sapper attack at FOB4 the previous August, when satchel charges had been thrown in the doors of the Americans' rooms, I contemplated sneaking quickly over and latching the door.

I never had a chance to carry out that action. There was a loud explosion and flash from the door. It sprayed me with fragments that bounced off the floor. Bryon shouted out that he was hit. Apparently, he had been sitting on his bunk pulling on his trousers when the siren started. I tried to get out from under my bunk but found something blocking me.

Damage to room occupied by Bryon Loucks and Joe Parnar on March 2, 1969. B-40 rocket hit and sheared off double two-by-four jamb to left of door, punched a three-foot hole in the Masonite room center divider, and left an eight-inch exit hole in the solid cement block wall on the opposite side of the building. (Joe Parnar photo)

I asked Bryon, "Are you against my bunk? I can't get out."

He said he wasn't, and I realized that the duffel bags from the shelves on the wall above us had come down and were occupying the space between our bunks. I pushed my way out and reached in the dark to find Bryon. He told me he was hit in the chest and said, "Stick your fingers in the holes, stick your fingers in the holes."

With the blood coming out he thought he might have a gaping wound. I touched his chest and found it wet from blood but felt no gaping holes.

Someone came to the room door with a flashlight and asked if everyone was all right. I had sustained some minor frag wounds in my left leg

Exit hole on the west side of the building. (Luke Dove photo)

and buttock but was okay. I told the person at the door that Bryon had been hit. A short time later someone else arrived with a stretcher, and we loaded Bryon onto it and took him to the dispensary, where he was stabilized. Besides being wounded in the chest, he had shrapnel in one of his knees. Shortly afterward, he was medevac'd to Pleiku.

When it got light I took some pictures of the room. The rocket had impacted at the door, shearing off the double 2x4 jamb. The shape charge then punched a hole through the Masonite partition between our room and the team room on the other side of the building. The

Inside room after RPG strike. Blood on Joe Parnar's bed sheet. (Joe Parnar photo)

rocket exited by making an eight-inch hole through the four-foot-high, solid-cement-block outside wall. The story I heard was that someone in that room was bending over putting on his boots while sitting on a bunk and narrowly missed being decapitated. The mattress on my bunk had been shredded in a half-dozen places by large fragments, and I was certainly glad I had not been on it when the rocket hit. John Walton was lucky he was still at his poker game when the attack occurred. He would have been seriously wounded if he had been in the bunk above mine, and there wasn't room for both of us under my bunk.

John Walton outside the room hit by the B-40 RPG. Standing next to newly replaced wall and doorway. (John Peters photo)

A work crew repaired the damage that same day, and by nightfall you couldn't tell the room had been hit except for the bulge in the corrugated metal roof above the door. As a result of the attack, I must admit I was uncomfortable sleeping in the room for the rest of my time at CCC. I figured the enemy may have set up aiming sticks outside the compound and could hit the room any time they wanted. I slept in a bunker on the wall the next night, but it was so uncomfortable that I decided to go back to the room after that. Walton took Loucks's bunk, which helped to reassure me somewhat. He said that the odds of a rocket hitting the exact same location twice were probably not very good. I only had to sleep there a couple more weeks anyway, since I had my R&R to use and would be away for at least a week of my last month in Vietnam.

◊ ◊ ◊

I was flying chase medic the day we extracted the body of 1st Lt. James L. Ripanti from southern Laos. I remember the general area was south of the landmark known as the Falls and south of the combined Highways 96/110. The word we got from the team on the ground was that one of their straw hat team members had taken a round in the chest and was not breathing. Since the team could not reach an LZ where the helicopter could land, the extraction was made by McGuire rig.

After the chopper lifted Ripanti out, the remainder of the team continued their mission, perhaps searching for an LZ for extraction. We flew to Leghorn because it was closer than Ben Het.

At Leghorn, the pilots eased Lieutenant Ripanti's body onto the helipad and we landed after those at the site had removed it from the strings. They then loaded him onto our chase slick and I felt for a pulse. But there was none. His body was already cold. Apparently, the chilly ride for 15 to 20 minutes had really had a cooling effect.

We flew his body back to Dak To. With only about three weeks until DEROS, I was ready for some R&R and ready to go home.

◊ ◊ ◊

On March 15, 1969, a roadblock mission composed of a company of Montagnard soldiers was inserted into southern Laos. A napalm strike inadvertently hit some of the men in perimeter positions, killing three Montagnards and seriously burning five others. I was the chase medic on the Huey slick that flew over the opening within the roadblock company's perimeter and descended into the LZ. Several AKs opened up on the ship, and I heard a round strike it with a bang.

The pilot dipped the nose of the helicopter and increased airspeed while the door gunners and I returned fire. We pulled out of the area and gained altitude. I had less than a month to go in-country and it seemed the closer to DEROS I got, the hairier things were becoming.

I was about to light a cigarette after we had regained altitude when I realized my ass was wet. I looked down to check if I was hit and bleeding and saw a stream of fuel coming from under the door gunner's seat. The pulsating beat of the rotor blades made it look like a series of waves rolling across a beach. Without trying to so much as move, I flicked the cigarette and the matches out the door. I got the door gunner's attention and pointed to the fuel. I then saw him talking into his headset mouthpiece advising the pilots of the situation.

He motioned for me to hand him one of the blankets I had brought with me to keep the wounded warm so that he could use it to plug the hole where the fuel was coming out. I suddenly remembered somewhere from my chemistry classes that certain fibers can combust when exposed to certain chemicals, and I asked the door gunner to confirm with the pilots that this was not going to happen. He said it was OK so I gave him the blanket, which he stuffed against the hole and held in place with his foot.

I didn't take my eyes off the ship's fuel gauge for the rest of the ride back to Dak To. After we landed and I got off the chopper, I discovered that my fatigue pants were soaked in fuel. Since there were still several wounded to extract, I was directed to another slick in order to complete the mission. At that moment, if there would have been a backup medic at Dak To and I had $500 in my pocket, I would have offered it to him to take my place. I was very scared and shaken.

Since there was no medical backup, I got on another helicopter and flew back into Laos to medevac the wounded. The second time in, the ship did not take any shots because air strikes in the meantime had suppressed the enemy fire.

We picked up the five burned Montagnards, and it was quite crowded on the chase ship on the ride back. I was concerned about fluid loss from the man with the worst wounds, as he had large water blisters over his chest as a result of the burns. I decided to put an IV in him to keep his blood pressure up. The Montagnard's leg was extended close to me, and I opted to put the IV in a vein in his leg rather than make everyone move so I could get at his arm. I tried to get the needle into a vein but had no luck. I removed it and tried again. My first thought was that he must be in shock. It occurred to me when I was going to stick him a third time that I was doing it the wrong way. I was trying to insert the needle against the direction of blood flow in the vein. Feeling like a real ass, I turned the needle in the other direction and hit the vein on the first try. I realized my nerves were so shot that I wasn't thinking clearly. After landing, I turned in the wounded at the 4th Division medical facility at Dak To.

These missions were the last times I flew chase medic at CCC.

CHAPTER 23

Other Lasting Memories of a SOG Medic

This chapter is an olio of incidents and recollections that because of my fading memories over the decades do not fit neatly into the chronology of my personal history during my year in Vietnam. These events happened at some point in the 1968–69 time-frame. Some are humorous, some gruesome, but I feel they are noteworthy in portraying my Vietnam experience.

◊ ◊ ◊

Sfc. John Probart was the supervisor of the dispensary at FOB2/CCC during my tour and there were occasions when our actions were civic in nature. Several times, John had me accompany him and we distributed excess medical supplies to hospitals in the Kontum area. Approximately a mile from our compound, French nuns ran a leprosarium that catered to Montagnards. I found these visits useful and educational. It gave me the opportunity to see how these patients were being cared for. Leprosy was, at the time, treated with dapsone, which was also one of the drugs we used as a malaria preventative.

I was impressed by the dedication of the French nuns and by the cleanliness of the facility. When a Montagnard was admitted to the leprosarium, he moved there with his entire family; thus the compound resembled a small village. This encouraged those who had contracted leprosy to stay for treatment, as many had families to look after. The nuns raised swine as a food source, and the sties had concrete floors that

Pet deer kept by French nuns at leprosarium about a mile from FOB2. (Joe Parnar photo)

were hosed down daily. The swill from the FOB2 mess hall was trucked to the leprosarium periodically as food for the swine. The garbage was boiled prior to becoming slop, again emphasizing the nuns' penchant for cleanliness. I also had a firsthand opportunity to see the insidious effects of the disease—several of the Montagnard lepers were missing fingers and toes that had literally rotted off their bodies.

One of my photographs from Vietnam is of a small Vietnamese deer that was kept as a pet by the nuns. It was kept penned up in front of the main hospital building.

◊ ◊ ◊

Another facility we assisted in the Kontum area was a hospital for Montagnards run by Dr. Pat Smith, an American M.D. from the Seattle area and a graduate of the University of Washington Medical Hospital. After completion of her medical studies she was inspired to open the hospital in Kontum City that was staffed mostly by Europeans and volunteers. She has been compared to Mother Teresa.

On one occasion, John Probart and I were delivering a bottle of oxygen needed for a child suffering from pneumonia. John stressed to me that I be particularly cautious about how I acted at the hospital, as a few of our predecessors had tried to impress some of the European women who worked there as volunteers by acting macho. Dr. Smith had written an unfavorable article concerning the incident, and it had been reported in some American publication back home. It demonstrated to me how one bad action could cancel out many good humanitarian deeds.

◊ ◊ ◊

Several procedures that we performed at the dispensary were not covered in great detail by the training we'd had in the States. One of these was the preparation of blood slides used in the diagnosis of malaria. I had watched Bill Lensch do several slides, and he showed me what to look for in the red blood cells. One evening, a Vietnamese civilian who worked for us was in the ward suffering from a spiking fever as a result of a suspected case of malaria. Bill told me to do a finger stick in order to get a drop of blood on a microscope slide and to prepare the slide by gram-staining the specimen.

I discovered that there were lots of tricks to this. After the first finger stick, I tried to create a smear thin enough to examine under the microscope, but I backed the second slide onto the drop of blood incorrectly and the specimen was useless.

Bill told me to go back and stick the patient again. I felt embarrassed because the man's wife was visiting him at the time, and I tried to make it look like two finger sticks was normal practice. The second time I attempted to prepare the slide, I failed to fix the blood by drying it over a Bunsen burner flame and accidentally washed the blood off the slide while trying to stain it. Once again, Bill told me to go get another drop of blood.

I went back, and the man's wife relayed through one of the Vietnamese interpreters who was present that her husband did not want to be stuck again because his finger was sore. I assured them that this would be the last time. If I screwed up the procedure one more time, I was going to tell Lensch to do it himself. I suspected he was getting a kick out of my ineptitude. Luckily, the third attempt yielded a usable slide.

The first time I conducted sick call for the indigenous personnel and their dependents, I concluded that our prior education had not prepared us for reality. When we had classes on diagnosis and treatment in Medic training, we usually worked on one case per evening and had all of our books and the *Merck Manual* available to consult for research. The doctors would supply symptoms and lab results from situations we had studied during the class.

In Vietnam I would have a line of sometimes 25 people waiting to see me. Through An, the interpreter, I might learn that a woman's baby or an adult looking for treatment had had diarrhea for the last three days. An proved to be my savior. After seeing me sitting there thinking for a minute, trying to decide which tests to have done, he advised me, "The other medics prescribe polymagma and Lomotil." I told him OK, and he wrote up the prescription and I signed it. It was then that I became aware that many of our diagnoses were incomplete and that our treatments only dealt with symptoms because of time constraints.

Probably the most appreciative patient I treated at the dispensary was an indigenous team member who hadn't urinated for two or three days. Lensch told me to catheterize him, a procedure for which we had extensive training while using dummies at Fort Sam Houston. The team member's skin smelled of urine, and he was in great discomfort. I could see the relief come over his face as I slowly released the urine from his bladder. After the catheterization, he was able to urinate normally again.

While working in the dispensary sometime in the fall of 1968, one of the Vietnamese who worked for the FOB brought in his nephew, a four-year-old boy named Hiep. He was suffering from a quarter-sized cyst on a gland in his groin area right where his left leg met his trunk. I cleaned out the cyst, which had ruptured, and removed a couple of cc's of cheesy white sebaceous material. I irrigated the cyst and put in a gauze drain. Hiep stayed in the dispensary for about a week while we cleaned out the infection and he recuperated. All of the medics got quite attached to him. He had the run of the place. During that time a couple of the medics who lived in the dispensary couldn't find their flashlights. It was later discovered that Hiep had taken them and stashed them in his clothes in the ward area where he slept. I don't know why he was so attracted to flashlights or what he intended to do with them.

◊ ◊ ◊

Another one of the duties handled by the dispensary was examining the prostitutes from the Green Door, a house of ill repute located a short distance from the north gate of the compound. This was done on a monthly basis. Venereal disease was quite common, and by keeping the girls disease free, it benefited the Americans who felt the need to relieve their combat stress by visiting the establishment. (I remember John Probart commenting that officers didn't get V.D. Their ailments were recorded as "nonspecific urethritis." I never did find out if he was kidding or not.) The monthly examinations gave the medics the inside track on which of the girls were clean and which were to be avoided until their treatment was complete.

The treatment itself was somewhat brutal. Because of the resistant strains of gonorrhea in Vietnam, 5cc's of penicillin would be injected into each buttock. The injections were administered for three consecutive days. If there was also evidence of the presence of a nonspecific disease, 1cc of streptomycin was added to the dosage. One of the girls, when asked why she didn't return for the second and third days' treatment, responded that it was because her butt was too sore.

It was while performing this duty that I witnessed the only occasion during my entire tour of anyone coming to the dispensary for medical cross training. I don't know why everyone shunned it so much. Maybe they thought they would be put to work changing bedpans. On one of the days when the girls from the Green Door were scheduled to come in for their monthly checkup, a half-dozen officers, ranging from captain to first lieutenant, arrived at the dispensary for cross training. Of course, they all volunteered to assist with obtaining the vaginal smears from the girls. I was working on the microscope examining the gram-stained slides for gram-negative diplococci, which indicated the presence of gonorrhea. I was somewhat embarrassed as the officers all gawked as they took turns obtaining the smears.

A case of military voyeurism at its best.

Several times on days when I worked in the dispensary, I was sent to the mess hall at lunchtime to stand at the door and hand out chloroquine-primaquine tablets, which the Army recommended be taken weekly to prevent malaria. A good number of the Americans would refuse them, claiming they gave them diarrhea. My thoughts about many of these refusals were, "Your diarrhea wouldn't have anything to do with all the beer you swill nightly in the club, would it?"

One humbling experience I had was when Sfc. Lou Maggio, another of our supervisors at the dispensary whose skills I regarded as close to that of a doctor, told me he wanted me to give a class to one of the Montagnard companies on the application of tourniquets. Lou sat in to evaluate me on my instructional techniques. I thought I did a pretty good job demonstrating on a volunteer while using an interpreter to relay the necessary information.

After I was done, Lou had the interpreter call up another two Montagnards, one to act as patient and another to apply the tourniquet. He then specified that the patient had a head wound. I had not made it clear in my instructions that tourniquets were to be used on the extremities only, but fortunately the 'Yard who was to apply the tourniquet hesitated as he had second thoughts about putting the tourniquet around the patient's neck. I learned not to take common sense for granted and to always be specific.

◊ ◊ ◊

The most gruesome thing I witnessed in my tour was after a recon team lost all three of its American members. A SLAM Company was inserted to look for the missing Americans when all communications with them had ceased. It took the company three or four days to locate the bodies and bring them back to the FOB in rubber body bags. When we opened the body bags outside the rear of the dispensary, I did a double take. The faces of the corpses were pure white and appeared to be moving. It took a few seconds to realize that every inch of exposed skin was covered with maggots several layers thick. We sprayed the maggots with GI insecticide, and as they sloughed off it was as if the faces were melting from a fire in a house of wax. Afterward, identification could only be made by body size and the type of weapon carried because the maggots had eaten off all the distinguishing facial features. One of the bodies was identified by the high school class ring on one of its fingers. We removed the classified maps, codebooks, notes, and weapons from the bodies, zipped up the body bags, and sent them off to Pleiku. I have often wondered how the corpses were cleaned up prior to being shipped back to the States.

◊ ◊ ◊

One of the days while I was working in the dispensary, I was told to deliver some medical supplies to the 'Yard camp which was three to four miles south of FOB2 on the road to Pleiku. I used our Jeep, which also served as an ambulance, to drive there.

On the return trip, I picked up a middle-aged Vietnamese man who was hitchhiking. This was shortly after a currency changeover of MPCs (military payment certificates) had taken place. MPCs were used as money by American personnel in Vietnam. They were intended for use only by Americans in the PX or in American clubs, and currency changeovers were done periodically because so many MPCs got into Vietnamese hands through the black market.

The man possessed a wad of the old, now worthless, MPCs and he held them out while pleading with me, "You can do for me?"

I told him, "Sorry, buddy, there is nothing I can do."

I imagine the changeovers had a devastating effect on the local economies.

◊ ◊ ◊

In early 1969, a fellow medic, George W. Bacon III, was in the village outside the wire, north of our compound. An ARVN truck struck an elderly Montagnard on the road and just kept going. George and another

Robert L. Howard (left) and Sgt. George W. Bacon, III at FOB2, late 1968 or early 1969. (Daniel Lindblom photo)

medic took the ambulance Jeep from the compound and brought the Montagnard to the dispensary to try to save him, but he was already dead. The next day the body was taken to the province hospital in Kontum, but the old man's wife showed up at the dispensary looking for money for a coffin and burial expenses for her husband.

The result of this incident was a directive that we were to take civilian casualties from the area directly to the province hospital and not bring them to the FOB. Only indigenous personnel, or their dependents who worked for us, could be brought into the compound for emergency treatment. I believe the FOB paid for the coffin and burial expenses for the old Montagnard, but all future cases went to the province hospital.

◊ ◊ ◊

The province hospital did not have a reputation of providing quality medical care. There was a Vietnamese civilian who worked for us whose job it was to clean the cut-down 55-gallon drums used in the indigenous latrines. He would drag the drums out daily and burn away the solid wastes with gasoline. One time the feces did not burn up completely, so he poured additional gasoline into the hot drum. The intense heat of the drum made the gasoline catch fire, and the flame went up the stream of gas into the gas can, which then exploded and burned him over 80 percent of his body. He was wearing only a pair of shorts when the accident occurred.

We covered his blistered body with some furacin gauze and put in an IV of Ringer's lactate because he was losing so much of his body fluids into the blisters. He was then transferred to the province hospital. The next day we received word that the hospital staff had let the IV run out and did not add another, and the patient died during the night. After that I felt sending the Vietnamese to the province hospital in Kontum to be treated was akin to a death sentence.

◊ ◊ ◊

Also, in early 1969 we were advised that a major general would be visiting CCC and would inspect the compound. I was given the task of representing the medic assigned to a Hatchet Platoon and informed that I would be reviewed by the general. We set up a display of the gear we supposedly carried on operations and neatly arranged it on a poncho with the rest of our equipment. I admit that I selected medical supplies that fit nicely on the poncho and not what I really carried on operations.

The day before the major general was to arrive, we had a rehearsal. Ralph Rodd was there representing a recon team, as was Ron Podlaski, who had come down from CCN to run recon missions. It was a hot day, so the officer in charge let us go into a small metal-roofed shed near the inspection area to get out of the sun while he looked over the displays. Ron was holding his CAR-15 and relating how one time shortly after an insertion, in anticipation of a hot LZ, he had fired off his weapon accidentally. He said he had a nervous habit of playing with the trigger. As he told this story, he had his weapon pointed up and kept playing with the trigger. Damned if he didn't shoot a hole through the metal roof of the shed. I had heard that accidentally firing your weapon in the compound would result in a $50 fine, but Podlaski lucked out. The officer in charge didn't do anything about it.

We all thought the incident was pretty funny.

A few days before the major general was to arrive, a 'Yard on one of the recon teams was shot in the shoulder. He had been lying prone and the bullet shattered his scapula and then traveled down the muscles of his back. We sent him up to the 4th Division X-ray facility at FSB Mary Lou to see where the bullet had lodged. When he returned to the compound, someone on the medical staff proposed the idea that if we put him on antibiotics and let him stabilize for a couple of days, we could be in the process of removing the bullet while the major general inspected the dispensary. Everyone felt this would really impress him.

On the day of the major general's arrival, I stood inspection as he reviewed our Hatchet Platoon. Afterward, I went over to the dispensary. I was told the major general had not even bothered to come there. It was just as well as they had been unsuccessful in extracting the bullet. Two medics had attempted to locate it and failed even after extending the incision another eight inches down the Montagnard's back. I gloved up and tried myself, but couldn't find it either. We sutured the wound and brought him back to the 4th Division for another X-ray. The bullet had moved several inches lower than where it had been three days before. It was now about three inches below the bottom of the eight-inch incision that already had been made on the 'Yard's back. One of the medics numbed the area using local anesthetic for the second time, extended the incision by another three inches, and removed the bullet.

I was amazed how much the bullet had traveled in just three days. But I learned that when you know where a bullet is, don't wait around and take the chance of it moving.

The Montagnard ended up with quite a scar, all in order to impress a major general.

◊ ◊ ◊

Another incident that took place around this time was when Hlock, the tail gunner from RT Ohio with whom I had worked the previous summer, came in to the dispensary with his four lower front teeth infected. The Montagnards had a custom of filing down their lower front teeth when they arrived at manhood. He had filed his teeth down to the gum level, and the gums were infected around the decaying tooth stumps. I didn't even need to numb him, as I was able to pick the teeth out of the gums with dental pliers. They were almost ready to fall out by themselves anyway. I gave him hydrogen peroxide to rinse his mouth out with to get rid of the infection. He was OK afterward, but I don't know if he ever realized that sometimes an indigenous custom was not all that beneficial to an individual's health.

Another time a Montagnard came into the dispensary complaining he could not hear out of one of his ears. When I looked in the ear with an otoscope, I noticed his eardrum was broken. When An questioned him, the 'Yard said he had had an itch in his ear and tried to scratch it with a bamboo stick.

◊ ◊ ◊

The medics, unlike recon team members, occasionally had to pull guard duty at night. On one of my turns, I was assigned as gate guard.

The duty required moving one of the old French armored cars the FOB kept on hand. The armored car was used to block the road near where the gates from the east and west sides of the compound met the north–south road to Pleiku. A .50-caliber machine gun was mounted on the open back.

When I tried to bring the vehicle to a stop in the middle of the highway, I discovered there were no brakes and so I coasted off the side of the road next to the dispensary. I had heard someone else had the same problem and banged into the dispensary wall and shook the whole building. I had a hell of a time finding reverse on the thing but finally got it positioned in the road where it was supposed to be. I shut off the engine and left it in gear so it wouldn't roll away. My duties now required sitting at the gate until midnight when the club closed.

Around 2200 hours, Lt. Col. Smith, our commanding officer, was returning from the club with some of his fellow Vietnamese officers. He was feeling pretty good and decided this was an opportune time to test fire the .50. He climbed up into the back of the armored car, aimed the weapon into the air, and fired off a burst to the southwest. The gun then jammed. He pulled the slide, chambered another round, and fired another burst. The gun jammed again. This continued for several minutes. I didn't really know what to do. I wasn't about to tell the commanding officer he'd had too much to drink and had to return to his room. Besides, I thought it was cool seeing the red tracers go shooting off into the distance. A short time later, Lieutenant Swain, the officer of the day, came running up and told Smith, "Colonel, the 4th Division firebase down the road is reporting incoming rounds."

"Fuck those legs!" was Smith's response. He told Swain to radio them back and tell them, it's "friendly" incoming fire. Swain returned to the commo shack and relayed the message and was told that if the firing didn't stop, we would be having some "friendly" artillery fire coming our way.

Finally, Colonel Smith got around to me and told me to go and find a go/no go gauge to set the head-space on the .50. I ran through all the recon team buildings, banging on doors and yelling in to see if anyone had a gauge. I couldn't find one but when I got back to the armored car, Smith was getting tired of playing with the machine gun and was chewing out Lieutenant Swain. He told Swain that the weapon had "damned sure better be operational by morning." Colonel Smith then headed back to his room.

◊ ◊ ◊

Another type of guard duty required walking around the perimeter of the base making sure the Montagnards hadn't fallen asleep. On one of my assignments, when I had been drinking beer earlier in the evening, I circled the compound and then decided to stop by my room and have another one. I sat back on my bunk and started to read a little but fell off to sleep. The next person scheduled to pull guard duty came into the room to get the radio we carried with us when I didn't show to wake him up for his shift. The next day the NCO who was on duty told me he had covered for me, but not to let it happen again or I would be fined $50.

On another occasion, I was into a heavy beer drinking session and the person on guard duty came to my room at 0200 to give me the radio. I hadn't checked the duty roster and didn't even know I had guard duty. I made the first set of rounds and went back to my room for another beer. I passed out on the bed, but luckily the next person assigned to guard duty came into the room at 0400 hours and got the radio for his shift. He later told me he thought I was dead because he couldn't wake me and my bunk was surrounded by empty beer cans. Once again, a sympathetic comrade saved me from a fine.

◊ ◊ ◊

Toward the end of my tour I was getting pretty cocky. One night in March 1969 there was an alert on the compound. Around 0200 the siren sounded to go to the wall. I was still pretty drunk from closing the club but managed to put on my web gear, grab my M-16, and show up at the wall in my underwear. Someone was firing a .30-caliber machine gun from the bunker where the road exited the compound on the south wall. Word came down it was one of our majors and that he was drunk. I thought to myself, "If he can fire, I can fire…"

I lay down on top of one of the bunkers and began taking single shots into the minefield that lay just beyond our position. I figured if I hit one of the mines, it would really liven things up. A new first lieutenant, who had been at CCC about a month, ran up and asked me what I was shooting at.

"The same thing the guy with the machine gun is shooting at, sir," I told him.

He began to reprimand me. "You're supposed to be setting an example for these Montagnards."

"Yeah, and the guy with the machine gun is supposed to be setting an example for me," was my response.

He then demanded to know how long I had been in-country.

"Ten and a half months. How long have you been here, sir?"

He didn't answer but told me to go back to the room and put my pants on. The next day I thought I might be in trouble, but no one said anything to me about the incident.

I noticed that punishment at the FOB was lax not only for me but also for others. An NCO once went to Australia on a seven-day leave and stayed for 30. When he returned, he wasn't court-martialed, just fined and busted down in rank to private first class. He was still the One-Zero of his team. It never occurred to me at the time, but I believe the nature of our missions and unit made it hard for the Army to punish wrongdoing. How could the Army court-martial an individual for being AWOL from a unit that didn't exist? People who are court-martialed in the military have the right to legal counsel. The fear that sensitive issues would arise and classified information might come out during the procedures must have saved us in many instances.

I would like to clarify the relationship between the officers and enlisted personnel lest my bad experiences with Lieutenant Rocky and Captain Gayol be seen as typical. We had many fine officers at FOB2/CCC who were greatly respected by the enlisted personnel.

The lieutenant colonels who commanded the compound while I was there were never a problem for anyone I knew. I always figured they were too high-ranking to be concerned with the enlisted men, especially a specialist like myself. If any one of us needed disciplinary action, the COs left those duties to the lower-ranking officers. I personally had great respect for Lieutenant Colonel Smith, Lieutenant Colonel Bahr, and Lieutenant Colonel Abt, the three commanding officers at FOB2/CCC during my time there.

Nor were most of the majors at the compound ever a problem for me or anyone I knew. Maj. Samuel S. Sanford is one I remember well, as he reportedly took a .50-caliber machine gun that he had mounted on a skid, loaded onto a Huey, and flew into Laos to shoot up trucks and other targets of opportunity. This was referred to as the "Stinger." Also, Major Sanford led the first of the roadblock missions, Operation Nightcap, in March 1969. He was the only major who actually led a mission that I can recall during my year at FOB2 and that made him all right in my book.

I found that the officers who had apprenticed on a recon team before assuming command proved to have a much greater rapport with the enlisted men. No doubt some of them found it a humbling experience to report to someone of a much lower rank, but it certainly endeared them to the rest of us.

One of the officers for whom the enlisted men had great respect was Capt. Ronald Goulet, company commander of Company B, Montagnard. Everyone spoke very highly of him. Captain Goulet would later be killed on September 26, 1969 while on a combat operation in Cambodia.

Nearly all of the officers on the SLAM and Hatchet Force operations in which I was involved seemed OK to me. Some of my favorite officers were 1st Lt. William Groves, 1st Lt. Lee Swain, and 1st Lt. Kenneth Snyder. These officers had not gone on the power and ego trips like some of the other first lieutenants at the FOB had. They may have gotten grief from the higher-ranking officers at the FOB for too closely fraternizing with the enlisted men, but that won them our respect. Even after the CO formed a separate "Officers' Club" at the FOB, they preferred to come to our club and drink with us.

Captain Ronald M. Goulet, Company B Commander, Hatchet Force. KIA on September 26, 1969. (Paul Morris photo)

Covey Pilots who stand out in my mind are Pete Johnston (SPAF 4) and Rex Hill (SPAF 1). Rex once flew his OV-1 out of Laos with the tail section dangling after taking enemy antiaircraft fire. It is a miracle and credit to his piloting skills that he made it back.

CHAPTER 24

Leave, R&R, and Home

In February 1969, someone I first met around Christmas 1968 asked me if I had taken my seven-day leave. George W. Bacon III had originally been assigned to CCN after arriving in Vietnam about the same time I did. He was transferred to CCC late in 1968. We both were medics and quickly became close friends.

George was probably the most intelligent person I have ever known. When he went through Special Forces Training, he was the Distinguished Honor Graduate of his class 68-5. He had the ability to read something once and retain almost everything. Throughout training at Fort Bragg, when we had weekends off, nearly everyone would go to town to let their hair down. Not George. While I and so many like me were goofing off, George was taking lessons in Vietnamese from the sister of Madame Nhu who lived in the Fayetteville area. (Madame Nhu was the sister-in-law of the late president of Vietnam, Ngo Dinh Diem, and in the early 1960s she was considered Vietnam's first lady.) When I first met George in late 1968, he could speak not only fluent Vietnamese but also several of the Montagnard dialects. He was always a good companion to go with to Kontum as he could readily communicate with the local inhabitants. He used to tell me I should read fiction, like Hemingway's *The Old Man and the Sea,* but I said I didn't care to read about other people's fantasies. Actually, I did read some fiction but never would admit it to him.

After getting to know George, I could not figure out the Army's logic in assigning personnel. He was one of the best medics to ever go through Special Forces training, and they had him running recon. I, on the other hand, never considered myself to be that good a medic, but that's what they had me doing most of my tour. George probably ran recon because he wanted to and because he liked the danger and adrenaline high.

George had befriended Chuck Willoughby at CCN, and he arranged for the three of us to go on leave to Kuala Lumpur, Malaysia. Chuck and I would have a lot of experiences to compare, starting with the day he had driven me to the Pentagon where I had seen Mrs. Alexander and gotten my Vietnam assignment. George and I flew to Da Nang and met up with Chuck, and the three of us had a great time in Kuala Lumpur.

George and I toured the brewery where they made Tiger and Anchor beers and got to drink free samples for an hour after the tour. We visited the Batu Caves (we called them the Bat Caves), which have special significance to Moslems and Buddhists. The female escorts we had while in Kuala Lumpur told us that during Ramadan every year people would climb the hundreds of steps up to the caves while carrying weights hanging from hooks that pierced through their bodies. At the bottom of the steps was tethered a five-legged cow that was supposed to be sacred to the Buddhists.

Our guides showed us where we could buy tailor-made clothes of exceptional quality for practically nothing in American money. I bought a couple of suits, a dress shirt, and a dinner jacket for about $120 total.

We also took a bus tour around Kuala Lumpur and saw sights like the Royal Palace and the local zoo. We toured a Buddhist temple, where we had to remove our shoes when we entered. I really enjoyed being with George, as he always wanted to do something interesting and didn't care just to hang around the hotel getting drunk.

It felt strange being away from CCC, and the war seemed very far off. After seven days relaxing, we returned to Vietnam through Da Nang. George and I parted company with Willoughby then returned to Kontum.

Around the beginning of March, George asked me if I had my R&R coming to me. I explained to him I had used it to go on the prisoner snatch attempt with Rodd. George laughed and said they couldn't charge me my R&R for going out on a mission, but I refused to go and ask for it. George said he would do it, and when he returned he told me everything was taken care of and we could go somewhere together.

Somehow it seemed OK for George to ask for my R&R, even if I had too much foolish pride to do it myself. I figured a deal was a deal.

We left Kontum at the end of March, again passing through Da Nang. George had a lot of friends at CCN, and we spent a couple of days there before traveling on to Hong Kong. We were put up on the CCN compound right below Marble Mountain. George showed me around and I met a lot of new people.

George had been at CCN during the sapper raid in August 1968. It was the worst day in the history of Special Forces, with 17 Americans killed. He had been running recon out of Phu Bai and was at CCN for promotion board at the time. The only soldier from FOB2 who was killed in the attack, 1st Lt. Paul Potter, had also gone there for promotion board. George was shot through the right chest and shoulder area and still had a large scar. He showed me the latrine where a couple of sappers were killed the morning following the attack.

During one of the nights we slept at CCN, a 122mm rocket exploded on the beach not far from our room. Once again, I noted the sand sprinkling down on the metal roof of the building. Someone said the rocket had been fired at us from up on Marble Mountain. I was glad it didn't hit the Marine Corps fuel depot located right next to CCN.

Despite everything, George and I were there to relax. We went with some others to the beach outside the wire and swam and tried surfing, but the breakers were only a foot and a half high and nobody could catch a wave.

While we were at the R&R center for our flight to Hong Kong, there was a copy of the *Stars and Stripes* newspaper, dated Sunday, March 2, 1969, that had an article about the wiretap recovery mission I was on in February in Cambodia titled "Pilot Wins 11 Hour Poker Game in the Sky." Of course, the incident was described as taking place in Vietnam. George and I laughed at the fact that no mention was made that the NVA guns were in Cambodia.

He and I both had specific reasons why we wanted to go to Hong Kong. George wanted to buy a camera with a telephoto lens to take pictures of birds at the wildlife sanctuary near his home in Old Lyme, Connecticut. I wanted to get a Rolex watch at the China Fleet Club where prices were duty free. The watch cost roughly half of what it would have cost in the States. George purchased his camera and after he got home, made a mount like a gunstock so he could take pictures while aiming the camera like a rifle.

Once again George was great fun, and we walked all around Kowloon and Hong Kong. We drank in the evenings at a British bar near the Star Ferry and met a British soldier who was assigned to the 5th Gurka Transport. George got up early one morning to watch a British officer inspect the Gurka troops. He was quite impressed. We left Hong Kong after five days and returned to Da Nang.

When we arrived, I only had about one week left until DEROS, and George convinced me to go to Saigon with him for a few days. He talked to some Vietnamese pilots who were flying a C-47 there and we hitched a ride. On the ride, one of the two engines conked out, and I was thinking to myself that it would be ironic if we crashed into the ocean after surviving a year in Vietnam. The pilots were able to make an emergency stop in Cam Ranh Bay, however. George arranged to get us on another plane and we made it safely to Saigon.

At SOG headquarters, we met Captain Lesesne, who was now working there. There were no hard feelings about what had happened between us previously when he was in charge of recon at FOB2. He even gave us some of his fellow officers' shirts to wear so he could take us to the Officer's Club in Saigon. I got to be a captain for the evening. We had a great meal, and the next day I had a hangover from all the wine we drank. I wondered what the penalty would have been if we had been caught impersonating officers?

Of course, George had another reason for going to Saigon. We both went to the Air America offices in Saigon to see if we could get employment. We had heard through the rumor mill at the club at CCC that they hired Americans to kick bundles out the door of planes flying "dynamite" runs into Laos. We had also heard they paid $11,000 to $12,000 for this kind of job. But when we talked to the personnel manager, he said they were now hiring Vietnamese for these positions since they could pay them considerably less.

While we were visiting SOG headquarters in Saigon, I got to see something I had long heard about but wasn't sure really existed—an actual human skull wearing a Green Beret that was mounted above the entrance. When MACV-SOG was created, someone had come up with an unofficial patch that showed a skull, blood dripping from its fangs, wearing a Green Beret. Behind the skull was a black and yellow bomb burst with a crossed AK-47 and a CAR-15 beneath it. The commanders of the FOBs tolerated the use and wearing of the patch on the compounds, but nowhere else because the significance of the symbols was classified top secret, as was MACV-SOG's very existence.

Also working at SOG headquarters was someone else I knew from FOB2—1st Sgt. Lionel (Choo-Choo) Pinn. He invited George and me to attend a Decader Club (originally a club for persons who had been in Special Forces for 10 years) party being thrown by Rocky Nesom, who was ex-SF and now an Air America pilot. Rocky and Choo-Choo lived in an old French villa in Saigon. It was a real mansion with marble floors, and they had several servants. Because George and I had decided not to pack the cheap civilian shoes we had bought in Kuala Lumpur and left them behind in Hong Kong, we wore our jungle boots to the party and looked really out of place. There were State Department people in attendance and everyone else was dressed in tuxedos and evening gowns—and there we were in our boots, blue jeans, and civilian shirts. No one seemed to mind our appearance and everyone was quite friendly. Shrimp cocktail was being served with the shrimps skewered with toothpicks onto large aluminum foil balls. George and I ate the shrimp off one entire ball all by ourselves. There was all the booze you could drink, and I woke up the next day with a Scotch hangover.

After Saigon, George and I returned to Kontum. I only had three more days to go until DEROS by then, and my final hours at CCC were spent with mixed feelings. I was glad to be heading home but melancholy too, because I would be leaving all the friends I had made. Since I felt I was still needed at the dispensary, it was almost as if I was running out on my buddies. Rodd and Worthley had gone back to the States on their extension leaves, and I never got to say good-bye to them. Several of my other close friends were out running recon missions, so there was no one to really celebrate my DEROS with.

A month before, I had been offered a $2,000 bonus if I re-enlisted. I thought about it, but was not impressed by the amount of money, as I still had misconceptions that CIA people were making tens of thousands of dollars for doing the same kind of work we were doing. But if the commanding officer of CCC had come to me at the last minute and asked me to stay, I probably would have done it in a flash—even though I had a feeling that if I remained in Vietnam, I would be killed. I realized how lucky I had been but figured my luck would eventually run out. I also understood the job of chase medic well enough that I knew I would take whatever risks presented themselves and do the job right, and that would only increase my chances of getting killed.

Going home was made a little easier as John Walton and Ron Brown were leaving CCC on the same flight with me. The out-processing at Nha Trang at the 5th Group headquarters consisted mainly of being debriefed and signing non-disclosure statements. At the debriefing, those of us who participated in Special Projects were told again that our cover story was that we had trained Montagnards during our tours. We were ordered not to discuss SOG or its activities and were required to sign a document that threatened a $10,000 fine, 10 years in jail, or both if we disclosed any sensitive classified information. At the time, the very existence of SOG was still classified top secret.

After Nha Trang, we were trucked to Cam Ranh Bay for further out-processing and given scheduled dates for our flights back to the States.

The flights of John Walton, Ron Jungling, and Ron Podlaski were scheduled the day before mine and Ron Brown's. We made plans to reunite in Seattle after discharge and party for a day or two before heading home. I was broke at the time and John Walton loaned me $80 that I was going to repay with some of my mustering-out pay when we all got together.

At Cam Ranh Bay, the Army inspected our baggage and took away the 37mm shell casing I had picked up in Cambodia. I could have put in the proper paperwork at CCC to bring it back with me, but never got around to it. I wish now I had done so as it would have been my only real war souvenir.

It was early in April when Ron Brown and I cleared the processing center at Cam Ranh Bay and boarded our plane for the flight back home. There were cheers by many as our plane lifted off the ground and we departed Vietnam. I actually felt a bit sad, though, knowing that I was leaving some of the best friends I would ever have. The plane stopped for refueling in Hawaii. When we got off the plane, some dropped to their knees and kissed the ground, happy to be back in the World. The Army went through our bags one more time, but the only thing they were concerned about was that I had not sharpened the top edge of my Buck General knife. I was permitted to bring it home.

Mustering out at Fort Lewis, Washington, took a couple of days, and Ron Brown and I were required to get haircuts and a new set of green Army uniforms. The haircut was one final bit of harassment prior to being discharged. The new uniforms were a complete waste of money. I never wore mine again after I got home.

When Brown and I got to the previously agreed-upon hotel in Seattle, we asked for Ron Jungling and were told he had checked out earlier that morning. We assumed Walton and Podlaski had done the same. I wished at the time I had gotten Walton's home address so I could repay his loan to me. The only thing I knew was that he was from somewhere in Arkansas.

Brown and I went barhopping in Seattle that night by ourselves. The last I saw of him was when we separated at the airport for our military standby flights home.

I had to transfer planes in Portland, Oregon, and as I was boarding, I was asked if I would mind flying in the first-class cabin because the stewardesses wanted someone to talk to. Since I was the only passenger in first class, I could have as many meals and as much booze as I wanted. I drank several Haig & Haig Pinches during the flight with two beautiful stewardesses pampering me all the way to Boston. It certainly was a far different experience than being spat upon, which some veterans describe as their reception upon returning to the States.

I took a cab from Logan Airport into Boston and then started hitch-hiking. I got a ride with a fellow who said he was only going a couple of miles down the road. We got to talking about the war and he drove 60 miles out of his way and dropped me off at my doorstep in Gardner.

I was home.

Postscript

For the most part, those of us who served in SOG honored the non-disclosure agreements we had signed. I always figured that failure to do so would endanger comrades who were still involved in ongoing missions.

The rumors regarding SOG I had heard at Fort Bragg prior to arriving in Vietnam proved to be accurate. In 1968 the casualty rate for SOG exceeded 100 percent—the casualty rate being determined by the number of personnel involved divided into the number of Purple Hearts issued. Fifteen Americans were KIA or MIA at FOB2/CCC during my time of service. In my 10½-month tour with SOG, I served with three individuals who were awarded the Medal of Honor: S.Sgt. Fred W. Zabitosky, Sp5c. John J. Kedenburg (posthumous), and Sfc. Robert L. Howard. Howard was one of the most highly decorated soldiers of the Vietnam War and received eight Purple Hearts. Over its eight years of existence, SOG personnel would be awarded a total of 12 Medals of Honor.

It was a privilege to have served with these men and all the other warriors of SOG.

◊ ◊ ◊

There were only a few people I served with in SOG with whom I had contact over the next 20 years. A month or so after I was discharged, George W. Bacon III called me from his parents' home in Old Lyme, Connecticut. George had also been discharged from the Army in April, shortly after me. He said he was returning to college and planned to attend the University of Massachusetts at Amherst. Before the service he had attended George Washington University in Washington, D.C. He even convinced me to go back and finish my education.

I returned to UMass in the fall of 1969 and lived in a dormitory. George was rooming in a rented farmhouse in North Hadley with a half-dozen graduate students. The next semester, I moved into the farmhouse when a room became available. George was taking skydiving lessons at Orange, Massachusetts, during that time and broke a bone in his foot on one of his jumps. He ran in a race for a veterans' group with his foot in a cast.

During the semester break in January 1970, the two of us went to Washington, D.C. George was to be tested for a CIA position he was applying for. (George always referred to the organization as the "Christians in Action.") He had gotten a lead on the job from Chuck Willoughby, who applied through the CIA recruiter in California. George urged me to apply when we were in D.C., but the personnel manager that I interviewed with told me the CIA only hired college graduates. I asked him about two-year contracts that I had heard the CIA hired people for, but he said you needed a college degree even for those. I didn't want to tell him he was a liar as I figured it might blow George's cover if they knew he had told me of his application.

George and I then went to Chicago to visit a couple of guys with whom he went through Training Group for Special Forces. Rudolph Schneider put us up in his apartment in a building owned by his parents. He was an ex-SF medic who was working as an emergency medical technician. Jim Whitaker, also ex-SF, was staying with Rudy and he rode back east with us. I dropped them both off at George's parents' home in Old Lyme.

George and Chuck Willoughby got the jobs with the CIA, and George dropped out of UMass halfway through the spring semester. They came up to Amherst to party a few times during the summer of 1970 while they were attending "plumbers' school," the term they used for their training. George told me what his salary was, and I realized that CIA people were not paid the huge sums of money I had envisioned.

I lost contact with George for the next five years. The last time I heard from him was in April 1975, right before the fall of Saigon. When I got home from work one day, my mother told me George had phoned and said to call him in Washington, D.C. He had left an operator's number, and when I dialed it, George answered and said, "Hi, Joe, how have you been I haven't got time to talk, but this is the deal. We are looking to get together a volunteer force of 400 men to go back to Vietnam and reorganize the South Vietnamese military. We can't afford to pay you anything because we want to show it is a voluntary effort so we can wrench funds from Congress. If you're interested, show up Monday in Washington at this address."

He gave me the address and hung up. At the time I was about to enter my second marriage and had a full-time job as a purchasing agent with a local company. I didn't go to Washington, and that is the last I heard from George.

It would not be for another 20 years that I would learn what happened to him. At the Special Operations Association Reunion (SOAR), John Plaster, whom George and I served with at CCC in 1969, told me he had heard George was killed in Angola in 1976. He told me to contact Robert Brown, editor of *Soldier of Fortune* magazine, for more information.

Robert Brown sent me a copy of an issue of the magazine from 1976 that gave the details surrounding George's death. It also provided me with a lead on George's parents, who no longer lived in Old Lyme. I have since talked to them on several occasions.

After leaving UMass in 1970 and finishing his CIA training, George became a CIA case officer. During one period, he served in Laos as a personal adviser to General Vang Pao, the leader of the Hmong tribesmen fighting the NVA on the Plain of Jars, in northern Laos. George was awarded the Intelligence Star, the third highest award for valor presented by the CIA. He had returned to UMass and finished his education and received a B.S. degree in political science, graduating summa cum laude, with a 4.0 average.

After my brief talk with George in 1975, he went to Angola in early 1976 and was killed by Cuban Communists in an ambush in February. He was the only American to be killed as a result of our country's involvement in Angola. I was deeply saddened when I learned of George Bacon's death. The world lost a truly dedicated, caring, and compassionate person.

The only other person from SOG I had any contact with after being discharged from the Army was Paul Morris, my teammate on Spike Team Texas. Paul was discharged in 1969 after I was, and we got together a couple of times in 1970. We went on a canoe trip to fish on the Moose River in Jackman, Maine, that summer. After that we lost touch with one another, and I would not meet anyone else I served with in SOG until I attended my first SOAR.

In 1992 I had joined the Special Forces Association (SFA) and the Special Operations Associations (SOA) and attended my first reunion with the latter in Las Vegas in 1995. I got reacquainted with several of my old friends and made several new ones. I finally got an address for John Walton and was able to repay my 26-year delinquent loan with interest. It was only then I learned that John was the son of Sam Walton, who had started the Wal-Mart store chain and was one of the wealthiest men in the world. Tragically, John died in a plane crash in Jackson Hole, Wyoming in 2005. John was big in stature, big in caring for his fellow man, and big in heart. He will always be remembered by me and many other SOG veterans, borrowing the words of the Jimmy Dean song, as a "big, big man—Big John."

Index